Powers of Reading

Lewis Wickes Hine, A "reader" in a cigar factory, Tampa, Florida, 1909 (Library of Congress)

Powers of Reading

From Plato to Audiobooks

Peter Szendy

Translated by Olivia Custer

ZONE BOOKS · NEW YORK

2025

Printed in the United States of America.
Distributed by Princeton University Press,
Princeton, New Jersey, and Woodstock, United Kingdom.

Originally published as *Pouvoirs de la lecture: De Platon au livre électronique*
© Editions La Découverte, Paris, 2022

Library of Congress Cataloging-in-Publication Data

Names: Szendy, Peter, author. | Custer, Olivia, 1966- translator.
Title: Powers of reading : from Plato to audiobooks / Peter Szendy ;
    translated by Olivia Custer.
Other titles: Pouvoirs de la lecture. English
Description: New York : Zone Books, 2025. | Includes bibliographical refer-
    ences. | Summary: "Reading, be it silent or loud, be it addressed to
    oneself or to another, is the site of entangled power relations: it is the
    micropolitics of the distribution of voices" — Provided by publisher.
Identifiers: LCCN 2024011398 | ISBN 9781942130963 (hardcover) |
    ISBN 9781942130970 (ebook)
Subjects: LCSH: Reading — Philosophy.
Classification: LCC Z1003 .S95813 2025 | DDC 306.4/8801 — dc23/eng/20240809
LC record available at https://lccn.loc.gov/2024011398

Contents

Readers and Readees

There is a lot of talk about readers. Considerable concern is shown for them, for how they read, how much, on what media, and what, and why. There is also plenty of attention to their age, their gender, their origins, their future, their predicted disappearance, their reinvention or renaissance. There are efforts to support them or awaken them when it is feared they are flagging or giving up, efforts such as Emmanuel Macron's declaration, in 2021, that reading would be the "great national cause" for the following year. Or Joe Biden's solemn proclamation, on Read Across America Day in 2022, that "reading ignites imagination, insight, and inspiration."[1] Throughout the world, there are plenty of equivalents to these encouragements to read, these mobilizations for readers of whom it is supposed that their motivation is dwindling: consider initiatives such as, for instance, World Book Day, which is celebrated in many countries (generally on April 23, the anniversary of the deaths, notably, of Cervantes and Shakespeare).

It seems, then, that *readers* attract no end of attention. Those who are never mentioned are the *readees*.

There is good reason for this: search as one may through all possible dictionaries, they are not to be found. French does not even have an equivalent for the English term "readee," which, although not yet recognized by the *Oxford English Dictionary*, is nonetheless regularly used in the tarot lexicon to refer to the one for whom the cards are read. More rarely, the term is attested as signifying the addressee of reading in general. We owe one of those occurrences to the American historian William Hickling Prescott, who suffered from serious vision problems and was forced to appeal to a reader in order to be able to read—that is, to listen to someone reading—the documents he needed for his research on the history of Spain. In the summer of 1827, he confides to his biographer: "My excellent reader...reads to me in Spanish, with a genuine Castilian accent, two hours a day, without understanding a word." And he adds: "Which would you rather be, reader or *readee*?" The word "readee" is in italics to signal that it is a lexical invention.[2]

Barely nameable in English, almost anonymous in French, nevertheless, readees—the evidence is inescapable—are and always have been everywhere. For just as it is impossible to imagine a letter being mailed or any address without there being both a sender and an addressee, reading cannot take place without jointly involving the one who reads and the one for whom he or she reads. This structure of address in general, whose consequences for a conceptualization of reading we will unpack, is also what I undertook to examine through several works, for listening. The very idea that every act of listening is addressed—to the other, to the other in me—is one that has accompanied me for a long time. It is only recently, however, that I have found it necessary to adopt a term that obviously echoes *readee*, namely, *listenee*.[3]

Why are they forgotten, then, these readees who do not even have a name? No doubt because the habit of considering reading exclusively as a mute practice, confined deep down inside each person, pushes us to conflate in the generic term "reader" the one whose voice reads and the one who listens. I tend to think I am both when I read: it is I who read for myself. I am the reader and the readee at the same time, and hence the latter disappears, is diluted, loses its contours and the specificity of its role.

From Rabelais to Cuba

For a long time in the history of reading in the West, a distinction was instead made between readers and readees, even if the latter did not (yet) have a name for their action, which—I will come back to this—seems rather to have been thought of as a passion, a simple receptive passivity. In 1552, in the dedication of the fourth book of *Gargantua and Pantagruel*, Rabelais recalls that "our late King François, of eternal memory" (François I had died in 1547) had "listen[ed] to a clear reading" of Rabelais's books read by the "eloquent voice of the most learned and faithful Anagnost of this kingdom."[4] The word "Anagnost" is inherited from Greco-Roman antiquity: as we will see in the chapters that follow, the *anagnōstēs* was the slave reader who read for others. Here, it refers to the "king's ordinary reader," a position held by Pierre du Chastel, who read translations from Greek and Latin, embellished with commentaries, to the sovereign every evening in order to prepare him for sleep.[5] Since the term "reader" can lead to confusion (it can indicate both the one who reads and the one for whom one reads), there is clearly some advantage to using the ancient and obsolete noun "anagnost." This paleoneologism should lead, symmetrically, to a specific name reserved for the addressees, for those who receive the reading, namely, precisely, readees.

The distinction between these roles does not belong only to a distant and more or less forgotten past. Closer to home, in the second half of the nineteenth century, it was operative in cigar factories in Cuba, where *lectores* read for the cigar workers, a practice that spread to Spain and the United States, and to Mexico and the Dominican Republic. Araceli Tinajero devoted a remarkable monograph to these *lectores* and also conducted interviews with the last representatives of this beautiful tradition. One of them, Santos Segundo Domínguez Mena, eighty-eight years old when she met him in Cuba in 2003, had been a *lector* for sixty-five years. In a particularly moving moment, he explains to the author how, now that he has stopped reading for others, he reads for himself: "When I have something important to read, I put on my eyeglasses. I read silently while I get my lips unstuck. I have to pay attention to it, just as others paid attention to me."[6] The old anagnost who begins to read to himself becomes his own readee.

The practice of reading aloud in cigar factories is attested in Havana as far back as 1865. On January 14, 1866, the weekly newspaper *La Aurora*, founded by the cigar workers themselves, described the first reading that took place in the Partagás factory as follows:

> One of the young workers of the workshop, who sits among the multitude of laborers, who number close to two hundred, announced in a clear, resonant voice that he would begin to read a work.... It is impossible to praise sufficiently the rapt attention the other workers lent him during the half hour he read; then another youth...took up the same book and continued to read for another half hour, and so on, until six o'clock in the evening; at that time, the laborers left the workshop.[7]

These early Cuban anagnosts, as we can see, could read in turn, one after another. The *lector's* position, however, increasingly would be reserved for a single worker who tended, from then on, to become a professional reader, paid by all the workers of the factory. Whereas initially it rotates, the distribution of the roles between anagnosts and readees tends to become fixed.

A Politics of Readees

The fascinating history of the cigar *lectores* is punctuated by conflicts, prohibitions enacted by the owners of the factories (no doubt they feared that the workers might educate themselves too much), and strikes claiming the right to reading. Or to be more precise: claiming the rights of readees, that is to say the right to listen to reading while working. Sometimes, as attested by a December 22, 1903, article in *The Morning Tribune* published in Tampa, Florida, the choice of which books to read was so hotly debated among the worker readees that it literally became a matter of life and death:

> A fatal duel with pistols occurred this morning at nine o'clock...between Jesus Fernandez, a Spaniard, and Enrique Velasquez, a Mexican. Velasquez

is dead and Fernandez is not expected to survive the night.... A peculiar
feature of the case is that the trouble which resulted in the fatal affray arose
from a discussion of a novel by Émile Zola — "La Canalle" [probably the
Spanish version of *La Curée*].[8]

The journalist explains that for some time in the José Lovera cigar
factory, there had indeed been feverish debates about whether or
not the factory's *lector* should read aloud the novel in question,
which was perceived to be indecent. The article also reports that
in the past, a factory in West Tampa had to be closed "for several
days because of a strike growing out of the proposed reading of an
obscene book": "The women employees objected to its reading and
the management of the factory sustained them and prohibited its
reading. Many of the male employees at once went on strike and it
was some time before the trouble was settled."[9]

Generally, however, the readees' choice of texts was determined by
more peaceful electoral procedures. In his memoirs, Wenceslao Gálvez
y Delmonte, a Cuban exile in Tampa who was, among other things,
a literary critic and a *lector*, recounts how the collective choice — or
rather, the election — of the books to be read was organized: "From
the podium, the *lector* announces the names of the authors and works
that are up for election, and table after table, almost in the ear of the
worker, collects the votes as if a deputy were being elected. Immediately, parties are formed, determined by sympathies with the various
authors.... Many abstain from voting."[10] And despite this abstention
rate, as one would say in electoral analysis (some do not vote to avoid
paying the *lector* afterward, others to leave the choice of the text up to
him), the "explosion of murmurs" that follows the announcement of
the result attests anything but a blasé indifference to what, borrowing
an expression from Michel de Certeau that will accompany us later,
we must call a politics of readees.[11]

This politics is also intimately linked to economic stakes, as evi-
denced by one of the few existing documents in which we can hear
the voices of cigar anagnosts collectively making a claim. In their

statement, published in the daily *El Diario de Tampa* on September 25, 1908, they thank a certain "Sr. La Presa," director of a theater company, for "granting them free admission to all the performances of the aforementioned company." As *lectores*, the statement continues, they are in fact "the best 'megaphones' [*voceros*] or announcers for all the theatrical performances and other kinds of shows that are organized in the city," although they are generally "forgotten by entrepreneurs." And, they add, given that theatrical companies are "speculators," that is, they operate for profit, "there is no reason why we should be required to read their programs [to the workers] without the benefit of free admission."[12]

The Readees to Come

The *lectores* tradition seems to be more or less extinct today. However, the distinction between readers and readees that had crystallized there remains a structuring one in many other contexts. Less institutionalized, closer to the intimacy of reading stories aloud to children before they fall asleep (like François I), there are, for example, reading services: Michel Deville staged this in 1988, in *The Reader* (a film adaptation of Raymond Jean's eponymous novel), and more recently, Mexican writer Fabio Morábito evokes it beautifully in *Home Reading Service*, a novel in which the narrator, sentenced to community service, makes his reading voice available to an invalid, a wheelchair-bound singer, or a sleepy colonel. He does so in order that they may read, that is, listen to him read. And the two roles — to read or to listen to reading — are here all the more distinct because, contrary to those who listen to him, this modern anagnost regularly finds himself "lost," reading on without understanding, as the words begin "to march around": "Your voice and head go in different directions," one of his readers says to him, to signify that he is only a megaphone, while she is all ears.[13]

From ancient anagnosts to the Cuban *lectores* and home reading services, this brief historical overview (which will be filled in, here and there, in the coming chapters) might lead one to think that today's readees are a mere relic, a remanence of more or less bygone eras. This is far from being the case. For if we consider the increasing number of audiobooks that are read every year, the readee's role seems more relevant than ever. It is no coincidence that in 2022, Spotify, the streaming platform, massively invested in this new market, which has so far been dominated by Amazon's Audible service. The current model is à la carte purchase; in the future, however, there may be different offerings, notably, some including advertising.[14] Just as the Cuban *lectores'* readings were punctuated by promotion of theatrical companies, so Juliette Binoche's voice reading in a recent audiobook, Marguerite Duras's *The Lover* (*L'amant*), could be interrupted by advertisements.

The audiobook is the result of a long history: after Cyrano de Bergerac's visionary anticipations, which we will glimpse later, that history will have begun with the use of records for the blind.[15] As we shall see, in an 1878 article, "The Phonograph and its Future," Thomas Edison explicitly considered this possibility. And in the wake of his predictions, futurological accounts of reading emerged that also anticipated the practice of networked reading. In "The End of Books," one of the stories in Octave Uzanne's *Tales for Bibliophiles*, published in French in 1895 and illustrated by Albert Robida, one is thus called upon to imagine a future where "nothing will be lacking" for the people who will be able to "intoxicate themselves on literature as on pure water," because there will be "fountains of literature in the streets as there are now hydrants": these will be "little buildings" from which "hearing tubes" will hang. Such pipes as will also be installed in houses or in "the public carriages" and "the railways."[16]

More than the anticipation of technical devices, which we tend to privilege when we look at these stories, what interests me is that they help bring the figure of the readee back out of the shadows. These readees, shrouded in a strangely disturbing, yet familiar aura, appear in a short story published in 1889 by Edward Bellamy (best known for his socialist utopian science fiction novel *Looking Backward: 2000–1887*). The short story, which appeared in *Harper's Magazine*, is called "With the Eyes Shut" and features readings that, as in Cyrano de Bergerac's *A Voyage to the Moon* or Uzanne's *Tales for Bibliophiles*, happen via "two-pronged ear-trumpets."[17] When the narrator comes down from his hotel room for breakfast, this is what he sees:

> A number of ladies and gentlemen were engaged as they sat at table in reading, or rather listening to, their morning's correspondence. A greater or smaller pile of little boxes lay beside their plates, and one after another they took from each its cylinders, placed them in their indispensables [such is the name of the devices in question] and held the latter to their ears.... Disappointment, pleased surprise, chagrin, disgust, indignation, and amusement were alternately so legible on their faces that it was perfectly easy for one to be sure in most cases what the tenor at least of the letter was.[18]

What becomes *legible* is thus the faces of the readees, whereas the read text is offered only through them, so to speak.

The Readees' Emancipation

What appears at the edge of this futurological horizon of reading, what threatens the future of reading while opening it to its opportunities, is the return or ghostly reappearance of the readees behind the readers who mask and deafen them. The massive (and long-anticipated or prophesied, as we have seen) rise of vocalized reading in the era of digital networks certainly allows readees to regain an important role in the general economy of reading. And yet it is as though their new primacy does not go with words, names, categories allowing us to begin to say it or to think it. As if, in spite of their de facto centrality, readees remained de jure confined to the conceptual periphery of reading practices.

Indeed, today, being a readee is a role that continues to be considered secondary, even tertiary, in the reading scenes we stage for ourselves. The role is characterized by passivity squared: somehow, it is thought that whereas the author writes and creates, readers only decipher and collect, while — worse yet — readees do nothing, that is to say nothing other than listen to what is read. To be a readee would be a bit like reading by derivation or by proxy, along the lines of the beautiful scene described by the English novelist Elizabeth Gaskell in a letter to her daughters in 1855: in an omnibus (in those days, they were horse drawn), she is sitting next to someone who is reading *Little Dorrit*, which she herself reads over the shoulder of this fellow traveler. And she complains that "he was such a slow reader!" She describes her impatience with the insane amount of time it takes him to get to the bottom of each page. "*We* only read the first two chapters," she concludes, emphasizing the first-person plural pronoun: she and her reader neighbor make up a team as remarkable as the one pulling the vehicle in which they read.[19]

Rather than marginalizing readees or even erasing them by forgetting them in favor of a reading that is closed in on itself or has retreated to the supposed intimacy of a reading self, it is time to reverse the perspective generally adopted with regard to the history and evolution of reading. One should not think that readees, after having been relegated to the background for the centuries when the model of silent reading prevailed, suddenly find themselves at the heart of the vocalized practices of reading in the digital age. One should instead consider that these practices bring to light what had only been hidden in an apparent mutism: when I read silently, whispering in my inner self, *I listen to myself reading.* That is, I am already an audiobook for myself. As the old Cuban *lector* suggested when he described what it was like to read alone, reading like this, I am the readee of the reader that I am also (or vice versa). So that reading always involves experiencing or being tested by a gap — a delay or an anticipation — of oneself with respect to oneself.

The gap that then opens up at the heart of the reading subject's interiority, the otherness to oneself that wedges itself in there (that has always been wedged in there), is the spacing from which a new politics of reading may emerge. It remains to be invented, to be reinvented. And the first step in this direction is undoubtedly to begin to be attentive to the readees, including those who inhabit each of us.

. . . have you started reading, dear reader, or are you about to start?

When will you have (yes, it should always be said in the future anterior), when will you have started reading this, this very thing that you are reading at the moment?

Maybe you are not yet the one who is reading, or maybe it is already no longer exactly you; who knows, it is reading in you and you are listening to the one who, in you, reads.

To read, to read in the infinitive, without anyone, any individualized reader, yet being the subject of the verb, to read as though it were possible to conjugate the verb the way one does verbs that describe meteorological phenomena, saying *it is reading* the way one says *it is raining* or *it is snowing*. . . . Reading is murmuring, here, on the threshold of the text that awaits that you lend it your voice or maybe, rather, that you recognize as your own the barely audible voice that is fluttering in the gray zone where reading is already afoot, already underway, like a movement that you would catch as it flits by.

This gray zone of reading is what we are going to explore together. This zone where there is anticipation (and therefore delay), tension that pulls the voice in a particular direction (and in the opposite direction), loosening it, to use a phrase of Thomas Hobbes's to which we will lend an ear, *loosened*, that is, unbound, detached from the text, because it is already ahead of the text or lingering behind.

You are reading, then.

You read t h e s e l e t t e r s , these words that rise in an intimate chant that only you can hear. We will be talking about that single or multiple voice; we will prick up our ears toward its enigma. Listen: it is not yours or mine, actually, nor his or hers. It is the barely vocalized voice of your silent reading. Perhaps it is the voice of the text reading (itself) silently within you: tacit reading (*lectio tacita*), as Isidore of Seville so nicely put it in his *Sententiae* (3,14.9).

You are still reading, youbind, youcollect theseletters and thesewords that your murmuring phrasing constantly transmutes into discourse. Until the moment — now? — when you lose the thread, you are distracted, attracted elsewhere.

Then you read without reading, thinking about something else. And that can go on for a long time, an entire page, before the moment comes to turn it

and you wake up, and you suddenly realize that you were sliding over the surface of the words, that you were mumbling them without lending an ear to them, skimming over them while taking off at a tangent.

As you start again after the interruption, you have to admit that the charm has been broken, that you have to start over, maybe start over a little earlier, find a way to get back into the flow, into the reading movement that had been carrying you. It has a delicate power, it is powerfully fragile, the thread of that voice that flows through you and carries you off, but is at the breaking point at every moment. You find yourself, then, still reading — your eyes rove over the letters — while you are no longer reading — I don't know what you are thinking of, what you are dreaming of. . . .

We will try to capture and think these tangential moments in which you are behind or ahead of yourself. It is there — we can feel it — that the power of reading plays out. That is where you, reader, are caught, torn, stretched like an elastic at breaking point between the two extremes of reading, reading as a mechanical reproduction and reading as an unprecedented invention.

I have always loved sharing my readings — as you do, I suppose. Or to be more exact, I find it fascinating that they are *already* shared. Actually, it is not so much that I love talking about them (that can happen), but rather that I am terribly enthused when I discover the trace of other readers that has been deposited or imprinted on what I read. The marks are sometimes unassuming, like punctuation marks affixed by the one who read before me, who came through ahead of me. I remember, for example, with some emotion, the wonderful moment I spent leafing through books from Jacques Derrida's library that had recently been acquired by and moved to the Princeton University Library. On many pages were scattered a light line in the margin or the bare underlining of an expression:

cursive traces of a reading rhythm (*un phrasé lisant*), as it were, with its almost invisible scansions. And then elsewhere I would stumble on a word or a comment. Among those, this one remains memorable: in his French copy of Giorgio Agamben's *The Time That Remains*, in the margin next to the sentence that condemns deconstruction to being only a "blocked messianism" (*messianisme bloqué*), Derrida writes, "you unblock! / you're out of your mind!" (*tu débloques!*)."

In sum: I like books that are annotated, highlighted, or underlined, those I find in archives or those I borrow from libraries (I have to make an effort not to annotate them myself), sometimes covered — and then it can be truly irritating — in colored highlights or layers of accumulated glosses by students or scholars anxious to reduce the book to detachable passages.... (Once, the first time I was invited to talk on the radio about my writing, I was surprised to find that the journalist had opted for this radical and literal solution: of the bound volume of which I was so proud, all that remained were a few pages ripped out and placed on the table of the show, in an approximate order, like a game of snakes and ladders in which one could skip a few squares in order to get ahead. What was the point? To save time, I suppose. I was shocked, all the more so because my radio host at the time was the head of a monthly magazine called *Lire* [Reading]).

Now that I read a lot of texts in electronic format, I sometimes come across other traces of readings, new types of footprints: in one work that I bought in the Kindle format sold by Amazon — *The Untold Story of the Talking Book*, an interesting study by Matthew Rubery of the talking book, its past history and its recent renewal — I came across a sentence (I cannot give a page reference because there is no stable pagination in ebooks) that caught my attention for obvious reasons: "Listening to books is one of the few forms of reading for which people apologize." Intrigued, intent on being able to return to it later, I was getting ready to highlight it (I have a whole palette available to do that) or maybe attach a comment bubble, a bit as though the sentence were to become a character in a cartoon strip. And then I noticed that it was already discreetly underlined in blue, by a dotted line. I clicked on the line, and this information appeared: "4 other people have highlighted this part of the book." My jaw dropped.

I don't know what intrigues, or exasperates, or frightens, me most in this report, which comes from who knows where between the lines I am reading: the adjective "other," which seems to imply, by anticipation, that I, too, am about to mark that same passage (but how do they know, and who are "they" anyway, I wonder, before pulling myself together and thinking that of course "they" cannot know, it's just a manner of speaking...), or the number four, which, written as a numeral ("4") seems to announce an open-ended incremental counting (4, 5, 6, 100, 200, 1,000...), a counter, a reader meter. It feels as though there has been a short circuit, as though someone has preceded me, as though someone has taken my place as the one to whom the trace of past readings was addressed, be it without an explicit address, in silent and anonymous ways: this trace reaches me now through the mediation of a database in which it has already been analyzed, counted, interpreted. I think to myself, What? I am not the only one who has noticed that this passage is important? What? There are already four, excuse me, "4" others? And how many other others to come will pay particular attention to this same passage, given that the simple fact of knowing their number is probably enough to increase that number? Unless a disgusted reader opts for a sort of strike, avoiding reading the passages that are promoted in this way by a machine that reads and makes read, one that definitely seems more like a data-mining apparatus than the glosses and marginal annotations familiar from the history of manuscripts and printed books.

The internal monologue that bubbles up in me, simple and tempting, all the more tempting for being simple, is already whispering this to me: go back to good old paginated paper, to the *codex* that, after the rolls of antiquity (*volumen*), has reigned for centuries over the history of books. Do not be drawn in by digital sirens that call out to you in order to enmesh you in the databases of networked reading — a sort of social network of reading — where you will end up as a dotted line and a number (maybe you will be the "5" that follows the "4"), a mere variable for content suggestion techniques that await us and preconfigure our reading horizons. But then, another voice crops up in me, among the many voices that accompany and inhabit me as I read; this one says that this discourse should itself be resisted. For — and this is a question that will weigh on us in the pages ahead — haven't there always been machines and machinality in reading? Aren't there always machines that read and make read (that make one read this way or that way, that is to say like the "others," whoever they may be, and however numerous)? Weren't there already such machines back in the furthest antiquity, already in reading out loud or in a whisper, publicly, semipublicly, or, as Isidore of Seville so nicely put it, tacitly, that is to say in taciturn or silent reading?

We will cross paths with many machines and machinelike figures in the history of reading, starting with a certain slave we will meet in Plato, all the way to contemporary ebooks, via the mega reading machine that Hobbes constructed in and as the *Leviathan*.

Yet, dear reader, I digress. I wanted to talk to you about voice, about that voice that is neither mine, nor yours, nor his or hers.

If this book is thus also about a certain division of reading (*partage de la lecture*), that division is marked, as we will see, in the reading voice itself. For as I will repeatedly reiterate, that is where the power stakes inherent in the act of reading operate and also where they can be eluded.[1]

However, regarding this tacit voice that reads in me, infinitively, I have sometimes wanted to talk about it with other readers, to share the experience of listening to it. On such occasions, I have often been told that they did not hear it. So, in doubt — was I hallucinating? — I started to investigate, to look for proof, for tangible evidence.

When I discovered that it has a name in the neuroscientific literature on the question, I felt I had found confirmation that the voice
that I hear exists: in neuroscience, "subvocalization" designates the
equivalent of the inner speech of silent reading, although this tacit
vocality may not be constant (expert opinions diverge on that matter), and it would seem to diminish or even disappear when the
rhythm of reading accelerates (when one skims, as we say, rapidly
scanning a text).[2]

I do not mean, however, to appeal to experimental corrobora-
tion as though seeking to validate my hypothesis as a timeless fact
of nature. Mine is, rather, a historical hypothesis: if there is vocalization even in silenced reading, that is because it is an interiorization of the reading aloud that prevailed, as we will see, for many
centuries. And it is precisely by lending an ear to the situations of
noisy reading, whether ancient or more recent, that we will be
able to make out the stakes of the micropowers that operate in the
reading activity as though they had been swallowed, so to speak,
incorporated into our innermost beings. In other words, reading
always involves vocalizing a text for someone who listens, lending
one's voice to the text while a listener lends it an ear, even when I
am apparently reading alone. This does not mean to foreclose any
possible metamorphoses of readers to come.

This is why I will consider that the reading that arises in me
when I begin to read always already takes place in a scene that
mobilizes *at least* three actors: as I read, *I* let myself be traversed by
a voice that articulates itself for *you* even when it seems that *you* and
I are one with this voice that speaks for us and within us. And if I
am so attached to this minimal triangulation of reading (*my* voice
carrying *his* or *her*s to *your* ear, whoever or whatever *we* are), it is
because it would be impossible to understand anything about the
violence of reading or about its imperious temporalities without
taking into account these multiple actors that constitute its staging,
however mute and deeply buried that may be.

Indeed, how can we give an account of the reading imperative

("read!") that will most interest us, insofar as its inflexible authority accompanies (or even precedes) reading as it moves ahead or
opens a way forward? It is impossible to measure its impact, to
hear its effects, without taking into consideration the fact that it
resonates and diffracts in a little vocal theater, on the microscene
of power that plays out in us when we read. That is where this command to read, which is always presupposed, operates; that is where
it weaves and unweaves vocal tessituras. (It is presupposed even
in its very negation — "don't read!" — as Ulises Carrión, a Mexican
conceptual artist, understood when, in 1973, he inscribed a diptych
on two pieces of paper: "Dear reader. Don't read.")

In short, we will repeatedly encounter this categorical imperative (in Plato, and later in Sade and Kant, among others). We will
see how reading voices intertwine around this injunction as forces
composing a provisional equilibrium. Each time, this is precisely
where, following de Certeau, what we can only call a *politics of reading* is negotiated.

On the subject of this imperious imperative that subtends a micropolitics of reading, let me here share my astonishment at a series
of judicial rulings that I first mistook for jokes. It started with an
article published in French translation in *Courrier international*, in
July 2009, whose headline runs "Pire que la prison, la lecture" (Worse
than prison, reading)." The article discussed "sentence[s] to read a
book" that Turkish courts were said to have imposed since 2006. It
described, for example, the case of Alparslan Yigit, who, "sentenced
for drunkenness and disorder," had had his two-week prison sentence "commuted to the obligation to read for an hour and half a day,
under police surveillance." Questioned by a local paper, the offender
described a terrible ordeal. To the question "How did you feel the
first time you walked into the library?" he answered, "At first, it was
horrible. I had the impression I was being tortured and that all the

city's inhabitants were watching me and making fun of me." When asked whether he "really" read, he explains: "I started with a book about Turkish writers. I also read a biography of Atatürk. They were really big books. It took me a whole month to read them. Actually, I pretended, I just turned the pages. When I was told that the judge would quiz me on the content, I started reading in earnest. I would not wish that on anyone, not even my worst enemy."

Of course, I have no way of verifying this story. The only way of checking that this was not an inconsequential anecdote (or, worse, an invention) was to look for similar cases elsewhere, documented, if possible, in languages to which I have direct access. Since my fascinated surprise at poor Alparslan Yigit's story, I have found others. For example, in an article in the *Guardian* in 2017, I learned that a judge in the State of Virginia had condemned adolescents (who had vandalized some tombs, tagging them with swastikas and white supremacist slogans) to read thirty-five books by authors such as Alice Walker, Elie Wiesel, Toni Morrison, and Hannah Arendt.[5] Indeed, the court considered that the perpetrators of these acts of vandalism were "not understanding the seriousness of what they had done." In 2016, the Italian daily *Corriere della Sera* reported another story, this one involving a network of underage prostitution in Rome: one of the clients received a two-year prison sentence and, as reparations for the moral injury suffered by the fifteen-year-old prostitute, was condemned to buying thirty books for her.[6]

It is worth pausing for a moment over the terms of the sentencing by the Roman court on September 20, 2016. According to judge Paola Di Nicola, "compensating the victim with a sum of money would, paradoxically, imply that the accused continue to repeat, via payment, the same type of proprietary relations" as the one previously established with the young prostitute, namely, one based on "monetization" (*monetizzazione*). On the contrary, she continues, "the purchase of specific books, most of them written by women," not only "avoids the aforementioned risk," but also provides a way of "becoming aware of what Laura is worth" (the name of the victim was modified in the documents made public), that is to say her "priceless...dignity." The judge concludes that the victim, "deprived of the means of defending herself and of cultural alternatives, will be able, through her own positive and determined conduct, that is, reading, to appropriate these stories and analyses, to use them one day in order to unlock the possibility of expressing fully her own freedom and autonomy of thought and choice." At the end of the sentencing is a list of the books that were imposed (these included Anne Frank's *Diary of a Young Girl*, *Mrs. Dalloway* by Virginia Woolf, *Histoire des femmes en Occident* [History of women in the West], edited by Georges Duby and Michelle Perrot, but also works by feminist philosophers such as *To Be Two* by Luce Irigaray).

What do they say, these judgments that are injunctions to read, either explicit (in the case of the vandals in the State of Virginia) or implicit (in the case of the young Roman prostitute)? Actually, despite the apparent bizarre character of the legal ruling that attracted the press's attention, there is nothing too surprising in them. For what transpires in these various sentencing measures is simply the Enlightenment ideal as it keeps resonating from Kant to contemporary discourses on reading as liberation.

Kant, you will remember, defined the Enlightenment as the exit from a state of minority, tutelage, or of immaturity for which one is responsible. According to him, one of the conditions for escaping from this state is reading, or more precisely, the free exercise of public reason in a community of readers (what he called a "reading world" [*Leserwelt*]).[7] This same Kantian idea resonates in UNESCO's launching, in 2003, of a decade devoted to "Literacy as Freedom." In the inaugural speech at the United Nations headquarters in New York, on February 13, 2003, Koïchiro Matsuura, the director-general, adopted eminently Kantian terms when he declared that access to reading "frees people from ignorance, incapacity, and exclusion," that it is "indissolubly linked to the human rights agenda" and enables "the downtrodden [to] find their voice."[8]

If learning to read and understanding what one reads are thus, for several reasons, a matter of voice, voice, as we will see, is far from a simple matter: beyond the triangulated division to which I have already alluded, the reading voice is constantly interwoven with this imperative — "read!" — that accompanies or precedes, it. Yet as we begin to see, this injunction is not only the expression of the radiant enlightenment of (self)-emancipation. Or rather, if it is, it is so only insofar as the latter also has a dark, obscure side. As we will see with Plato and Sade, reading can also be slavery.

—☌

The recent condemnations to read constitute a remarkable prosopopoeia, insofar as they attribute a voice, that of the judge, to the reading imperative. Indeed, it is as though this silent imperative, buried in my innermost being — so close to what Kant called "the voice of reason" — suddenly appeared on the noisy scene of a courtroom, where it takes shape, where it is empirically embodied.

These situations in which the tacit or taciturn scenography of reading becomes manifest have a lot to teach us. The hypovoices that subvocalize in me when I read are suddenly, so to speak, amplified, megaphoned, booming out in a life-sized theater in which I can listen to them and analyze their power games, the balance of powers. We will therefore travel back in time to reverse the development that, from Plato to Saint Augustine and beyond, led to the practice of silent reading: returning to an era when a slave might have read out loud for us as he obeyed an order to do so, we will watch the implicit unfold, we will see it literally become explicit. We will observe the micropolitics of reading in a magnified version that will fully illuminate them.

And this is why we will also lend an attentive ear to the innumerable reading imperatives (they sometimes appear in softened forms as a piece of advice, a wish...) that appear in so many prefaces or addresses to the readers that we are. Each time, from

Michel de Montaigne to Friedrich Nietzsche or the famous Baudelairian appeal to the "hypocrite reader" that I am, we find ourselves already included, already inscribed in a certain configuration
within a force field that precedes us, that awaited us. We will also,
however, auscultate the places where, at the very heart of reading,
lurks a certain idleness of the reader, a nonreading or a not reading that has the air of a counterpower: it was insofar as eyes detach
from a text and lift up toward prayer that the reading practices of
mystics, for instance, were of interest to de Certeau, who saw in
them the promise of a reading tending toward its absolute, on the
verge of casting off from the page. And as we will see, Walter Benjamin was not far from suggesting that the most authentic relation
or the most respectful relation to books might be that of the pure
collector, who, rather than reading them or buying or selling them,
simply lets them be as they are.

For reasons apparently far from Benjamin or de Certeau's preoc-
cupations, some have recently defended the idea that in the era of
the globalization of literature, proper reading practice should necessarily accommodate a certain degree of nonreading as an inevi-
table, one might say arithmetical consequence of the sheer number of publications produced on this planet daily. The logic seems
unimpeachable and it should be taken seriously: if, with Goethe,
who was the first to speak of *Weltliteratur*, we call "world literature"
the unprecedented plethora of texts that each legitimately warrant
attention, how can we continue to justify the need for close reading of the same canonical passages, insist that they deserve to be
constantly reread, or devote time to gloss them or listen to them,
indefinitely? That was essentially Franco Moretti's question when,
in an article that became a classic, he makes the claim for distant
reading: "We know how to read texts, now let's learn how *not* to
read them."[9]

By declaring that careful reading (what Anglophones call "close
reading," a practice close to French *explication de texte*) was dead
or outdated and by advocating for a sort of indirect reading or a

reading that relies on other readings, rather than grappling with the text itself, Moretti acknowledges the infinite proliferation, the limitless increase in what there is — in what there *would be* — to read. Since it is impossible to read everything, let's delegate reading, let's read what others will have read for us, let's read by proxy and statistically, tracking occurrences, mapping tendencies, evolutions. This might be the only way to manage in the face of what Valéry, after Goethe, staged in his *"My Faust,"* that is to say the relentless overproduction of writings, the textual overflow that leads to the fact that "inch by inch, century by century, [is raised] a monument of the UNREADABLE."[10]

Is our little vocal theater in which the micropowers operate and are undone not destined to explode, to be pulverized, by the inordinate onslaught of everything that one should read? Given its globalized economy and ecology, isn't there something terribly anachronistic in wanting to think about reading today at the microscopic scale suited to a distribution of voices that belongs to an epoch in which there were only a few papyrus rolls being handed around? And above all, what could possibly be left of that old vocality when my reading is becoming more and more hypertextual, distant, or mechanical, when I click on links that take me from one text to the next or when I search for the occurrences of a word in a work that is thus more like a database than a bound and paginated book? One does not pronounce a click. One does not vocalize or subvocalize the pure movement of referral from one passage to another. When all that is left is a search engine churning, the inner voice is left behind.

Granted. Yet the question is probably formulated in the wrong way. Maybe it should even be turned around: instead of looking for what might be left of hypovocalization in the era of hyperreading, one should take the current disruptions as the context in which to ask what *will have been* the voices that *will have* constituted the public or private scenes of reading for so many readers over so many centuries. If there is indeed an atrophy of voice as reading accelerates (a point that remains to be proven), the least one can say is that this is part of a complex mutation: I still make silent speeches and counterspeeches to myself as I browse through Google Books; many imperatives, many mumbled pronouncements, often contradictory ones, resonate inside me, interrupting one another as I jump from sentence to sentence, letting myself be carried by the flow of this world literature for which the internet could be a metonymy. My experience as a reader is certainly not that of Phaedrus reading Lysias's speech to Socrates or that of the nameless slave lending his voice to the characters debating in Plato's dialogue titled the *Theaetetus*. And yet, the way their voices share the scene can teach me a lot about the way my voices are distributed in a reading that may well be hypertextual but is far from being voiceless. And vice versa: my vocalizing practices of reading might well, in return, throw new light on the immemorial phonoscenography of reading.

It is therefore perhaps not so much that my voice disappears as that the speed of reading increases. (How could I be sure of that anyway, since it was already only a quasi-voice, a silent voice?) As we will see, it is rather theirs, Phaedrus's or the slave's voice, like the voice of so many readers since, that could, in the end, appear to us as being already *a speed differential*: their voice preceded itself, moved ahead of itself, was also delayed with respect to itself; it contracted and slackened by constantly making room for some not reading at the very heart of reading, for distraction even at the points of the most intense attention, one feeding the other and vice versa.[11]

Nonreading, in sum, in which zero speed and infinite speed are conjoined or exchanged, has no doubt always been accommodated within reading.

P.S. I barely dare add more words to this introduction, which is already too long. I have a number of misgivings about inscribing them here and will do so in a smaller font, to try to avoid burdening you too much. For you must already be tired, dear reader, tired out by this verbose preamble, tired ahead of time by what will follow: so many pages, so much time, so much effort....

(Rest assured, you are not the only one to experience such fatigue. László Krasznahorkai, whose stories will tell us so much about the temporality of reading, addresses the reader of "Isaiah Has Come" in these terms: "Dear solitary, tired, sensitive reader...." And *If on a Winter's Night a Traveler*, Italo Calvino's novel, which we will read as a vast staging of sexual difference in the reading voice, ends with this question: "Aren't you tired of reading?")

If then, like me, you are tired at the prospect of everything there is to read (and even to not read or to hyperread), I imagine that you will readily share my weariness in the face of all these manifestos for this or that way of reading that seem to flourish, especially in the anglophone world. Each type of reading claims to wipe out the previous ones, move beyond their failures, put them, and their claims, in their place.

As we saw, the distant reading championed by Moretti claims to have surpassed the close reading that had prevailed until then. According to others, it is surface reading that should replace the symptomatic reading to which Louis Althusser was so attached: Reading, they say, will no longer necessarily be about unearthing what is hidden under the text, its unformulated presuppositions; rather, reading will involve paying attention to what is in the text, nothing more ("just reading" is the name of this way of reading that does nothing other than "just read"). Yet others challenge symptomatic reading not with a surface reading, but with reparative reading, which aims to move beyond a suspicious attitude to the text and rehabilitate a certain naiveté or surprise in relation to it. Distant, close, superficial, symptomatic, just, reparative: the list goes on. (There are those who talk about "uncritical" reading, or "mere" reading.)

Despite the relevance of many of the arguments made here and there,[12] it almost feels as though one has stumbled into an academic supermarket in which a scholar who must read for a living can choose between various reading practices as though he were choosing between various brands of low-fat or skim milk. These debates, these choices on which careers and reputations depend, sometimes seem like tempests in a teapot. Each of these modifications, which present themselves as revolutions spawning a new type of reader, seem, in fact, to revisit roles that the history of reading configured long ago.

Consider the distant reading dear to Moretti: to map the phenomena that he studies at large scales, such as the spread of English and French novels in Europe around 1850, he consults national bibliographical catalogues in order to cull statistics concerning the translations of these novels, their frequency, their speed. Or again, to support global geopolitical hypotheses about the birth of the modern novel as a compromise between Western influence and local components, he compares dozens of critical studies, admitting, sometimes with a good dose of humor, almost as though it were a sin, that "actually," he made an exception and "did read" some of the novels in question.[13] In order to characterize this metareading, which involves collecting and classifying data, Moretti proposed distant reading as a slogan, in contrast to the close reading that prevailed in literary studies in the anglophone world since the 1920s.

Yet if we take a closer look (dare I still say that?), the ideal of detailed reading such as it was celebrated by the New Criticism itself depended on data collection that was closer to metareading than what one would imagine a reading in direct and close contact with the text to be. I. A. Richards's *Practical Criticism*, considered a foundational work for *close reading* (an expression that makes several notable appearances in the work), presents itself as series of experiments requiring readers to take note of their readings of certain chosen poems:

> For some years I have made the experiment of issuing printed sheets of poems . . . to audiences who were requested to comment freely in writing upon them. The authorship of the poems was not revealed, and with rare exceptions it was not recognized. After a week's interval I would collect these comments. . . . I lectured the following week partly upon the poems, but rather more upon the comments, or protocols, as I call them.[14]

One of the first and most famous defenders of close reading thus preferred to rely on derivative readings, readings of readings, or metareadings. It is as though the distance of metadata already inhabited the proximity that claimed to be most immediate.

But distant or hypertextual reading, metareading, comes to us from even further back than the close reading it is supposed to oppose after a century. We will see it embodied, for instance, in Faust, who, in the course of an extraordinary scene orchestrated by Goethe in the second part of his tragedy, flies over millennia of world literature. And especially, we will constantly have cause to wonder whether, in the end, the way it is already the case in Plato, every reading

33

is necessarily both close and distant at the same time, a vocal (or quasi-vocal) interlacing of distancing and contiguity. For being a distribution of voices, reading is both transitive (the reading voice erases itself in favor of the voice that it reads—it disappears the better to let that other voice transpire as the voice that speaks) and reflexive (one can always lend an ear to the voice that reads rather than to the voice that it reads). If there is indeed a triangulation in reading (my voice carries his or her voice addressed to *your* ear, whoever or whatever *we* are), it is a triangle that opens and closes constantly, according to systoles and diastoles that precede and make possible any distinction between proximity and distance.[15]

A Strangely Familiar Voice

("The Sandman")

"Dear reader," he says.

This way of being addressed or apostrophized is familiar, isn't it? We have read this phrase so many times, encountered it so often, heard it rolled out in many tones, varied in many ways. We will soon find it surfacing repeatedly under some of its innumerable guises in Michel de Montaigne, Arthur Schopenhauer, Søren Kierkegaard, Charles Baudelaire, Friedrich Nietzsche, Paul Valéry, Italo Calvino, László Krasznahorkai....

But whose words are they here?

The speaker is currying favor with the reader. He would like to lead the reader to be well-disposed, kindly, favorably inclined (*geneigt*). With a certain passion, almost as though he were getting carried away, he turns to the reader — to us, then — exclaiming "oh, my reader!" (*o mein Leser!*) The narrator of E. T. A. Hoffman's "The Sandman" thus shares with me, as a reader, his doubts, his hesitations as to the right way to begin the story that he has decided to tell. Should he begin with the usual "Once upon a time..."? That is a rather bland (*nüchtern*) start. Will he plunge the reader straight into the action, in medias res? The narrator doesn't seem convinced by that option, either. In the end, he admits that "unable to find words that seemed to reflect anything of the prismatic radiance of my inner vision," and he "decided not to begin at all."[1]

Did I read what I just read correctly? "Not to begin at all" (*gar nicht anzufangen*)? But I have been following the plot of "The Sandman" for quite a while already! How am I supposed to understand that nothing has begun when I am almost halfway through the story?

Obviously, something has begun (how can we deny it at this point?) without, however, the narrator himself having done anything to get things going. They got going by themselves as it were, as he explains by engaging me directly: "Be so good, dear [*geneigter*] reader, as to accept the three letters, kindly communicated to me by my friend Lothar," he declares, signifying thereby that what I have read up to now is not his writing, that he has simply offered up for my reading a correspondence to which he contributed nothing.

Granted. That is no doubt what the narrator means to say. Yet why do I have a strange feeling that I cannot shake? Why is it that this passage seems so strange as it addresses me directly ("Dear reader," "well-disposed reader"...), as though I needed to be woken from a dream?

We need to backtrack a little in order to understand what is going on here. What have I read so far? I have read letters, three letters in which the correspondents evoke reading and tell each other that they should or should not read one another or themselves. In his first letter to Lothar, for instance, Nathanael admits that he "liked nothing better than hearing or reading."[2] In other words, Nathanael is our double; he is the mirror image of we who are readers of "The Sandman," we who passionately read the letter in which he declares his passion for reading stories like the story of the Sandman.

The second of the three letters is the one Clara writes to Nathanael. She begins by confessing a mistake, a destination mistake: she read something she should not have read, Nathanael's letter to Lothar. To be precise, she read what *we* just read, the letter in which Nathanael talks among other things about his passion for reading. "I should have read no further," she writes, but then immediately admits that she could not resist: "I read and read!" (*ich las und las!*)[3]

36

Thus, Nathanael and Clara, our doubles, love reading and cannot stop. Reading what we read (the story of the Sandman or the very letter we just read), they have preceded us in the reading. And when we are then interpellated as "dear reader" or "well-disposed reader," when the narrator says there has not been a beginning, we get the impression that what he is actually referring to is reading: the reading has not begun because it was already under way. No one began to read, because there was already reading going on, and there were already readers reading before we recognized ourselves as such or among them. The strangeness I felt when I read this passage comes from an impression of déjà vu: as readers, we repeat what the characters were already doing, that is, reading. This means we do not initiate our reading: it, our reading, which is not really "ours," comes back at us from a distant past, its beginning seemingly lost and erased somewhere in the characters' past. Thus, if Hoffman's story is indeed a scene of what Freud called the *unheimlich*, the uncanny, this perhaps plays out above all in the reading, in the act of reading.

Why?

—☙—

As is well known, Sigmund Freud attributed the uncanny in Hoffman's story to the figure of the Sandman, that frightening figure whose mention terrified children and helped to scare them into obedience at bedtime. For Nathanael, the terrifying character represented the threat of being deprived of his eyes. (He was told that the Sandman steals the eyes of children who do not go to sleep.) Freud immediately transposes this: "We shall venture, therefore, to refer the uncanny effect of the Sand-Man to the anxiety belonging to the castration complex of childhood."[4] It is this repressed anxiety that returns in another shape when Nathanael thinks he recognized the Sandman of his childhood — he had identified him as/with Coppelius, the lawyer who often visited his father — in a barometer salesman named Coppola, who insisted on selling him eyes, that is glasses.

37

All this is far from reading, especially if we consider, as we constantly will, that reading (even when soundless) is a matter of voice rather than sight. The Freudian interpretation of the uncanny in "The Sandman" insists on the visual or ocular motif, which is indeed preeminent in the story. Nevertheless, the importance of vision and optical instruments—glasses, the spyglass through which Nathanael watches Olimpia's window, her "strangely fixed and dead"[5] eyes—should not prevent us from lending an ear to another motif, one that may be less noticeable but is nevertheless just as recurrent, that of reading.

Indeed, as the story continues beyond the three letters with which it started, without, as we saw, beginning, reading returns repeatedly. When Nathanael returns home to Clara, he spends his time trying to convince her of the existence of the supernatural: "Early in the morning, when Clara was helping to make breakfast, he would stand beside her, reading aloud from all manner of mystical books." But prosaic Clara is not inclined to follow his wandering mind and does not listen: "If I drop everything, as you demand, and gaze into your eyes while you read, the coffee will run over into the fire." Nathanael, who wanted to launch into an uninterrupted reading with her, "clap[s] the books shut"[6] and retires to his room.

Soon, Nathanael will have occasion for uninterrupted reading to Olimpia, the automaton he has fallen for. Without necessarily following Freud, who sees in Olimpia "the materialization of Nathanael's feminine attitude towards his father in his infancy," we can take Nathanael literally when he says, "only in Olimpia's love do I recognize myself."[7] And when he reads to the wooden doll, it is as though he were reading for himself: "From the darkest recesses of his desk Nathanael fetched everything he had ever written. Poems, fantasies, visions, novels, stories were supplemented daily by all manner of incoherent sonnets, *ballades*, and *canzoni*, which he read to Olimpia for hours on end without ever wearying. But then, he had never had such a perfect listener."[8]

Her "fixed look" and her mechanical gestures are the grounds for

Olimpia being described three times as *unheimlich* in the story,[9] and yet there is also something uncanny in the way she listens to the various things Nathanael reads aloud to her. For Olimpia is perhaps, after Nathanael and Clara, the ultimate figure in which we, readers, find our own reflections in "The Sandman": we are so taken, so absorbed in the plot, our curiosity is so excited, that it does not occur to us to interrupt the flow of sentences. Like Olimpia, we simply listen continuously to what is articulated for us. Just as Nathanael did when speaking to her, we forget that what captivates us is only what we read to ourselves.

As an *unheimlich* stand in for us readers, as a double for both Nathanael and us, Olympia embodies the moment when reading forgets itself, the better to produce itself. Borrowing Freud's language, we might, however, ask: What has had to be repressed in order for reading to become some sort of purely transitive verb, in order for reading to become only an immediate and uninterrupted dive into the world of the text?

The answer lies in the particular feeling of vocal uncanniness, the intimate terror that grips Nathanael when, earlier in the story, he rereads the somber premonitory poem he composed: "When he had finished and read the poem aloud to himself [*das Gedicht für sich laut las*], he was gripped by wild horror and terror, and shrieked: 'Whose hideous voice is this?'"[10] It is hard to tell which voice this is. Does this horrible voice (*grauenvolle Stimme*) belong to the text Nathanael has just finished writing? Is it that of the text speaking, conveying what it has to say? Or is it Nathanael's voice as he rereads his writing out loud, lending his voice, his horrible, unrecognizable, voice to the text? In other words, is it the voice of what is read or the voice of the one who reads?

We will soon revisit this undecidability, this unsettling vocal ambivalence, in a whole series of scenes from Plato to Sade and beyond. Each time, what we will come to recognize will be the voice we have as readers; it is a voice that must be forgotten or repressed for reading to take place (it must be erased for the text to be heard through it) but that resists, that insists and makes itself heard, here and there, in its opacity.

As we will find out, it is paradoxically when the reading voice is interrupted that we notice it. (As long as it is reading, it disappears in the act of reading.) This is a voice that appears only when it disappears, a voice that disappears as it appears, a voice that is condemned to the intermittence of what we will call *reading points*. Marcel Proust described its oscillations in a few memorable sentences that will guide us throughout our investigation:

> Before lunch, which would, alas, put an end to my reading, still lay two long hours.... Unfortunately, the cook would come in long before lunch, to set the table; if only she could do it without talking! But she felt obliged to say, "You must not be comfortable like that, should I move the table a little closer?" And merely in order to answer "No, thank you" it was necessary to come to a dead stop and bring back your voice from afar, the voice within your lips that had been swiftly and silently repeating all the words your eyes were reading; you had to bring that voice to a stop, send it out of your mouth, and, to manage a respectable "No, thank you," give it a semblance of ordinary life again, the tone of communication and interaction it had lost.[11]

The reader's voice had to be brought back from afar. Returning from the far side (*revenante*), whether we notice it or not, the reader's voice always has that uncanniness that Nathanael's voice displays when he reads for himself.

All the reading voices we will encounter could be (Hoffmann would not argue with this) ghost voices, voices that will continue to haunt us.

The Anagnost and the Archon

In a letter to his friend Atticus, Cicero confides his grief: "My reader [*anagnōstēs*] Sositheus, a charming fellow [*puer festivus*], has died; and I am more upset about it than anyone would suppose that I should be about a slave's death."[1] Another letter, one Cicero received from a magistrate called Publius Vatinius, mentions a reading slave who had run away.[2] The anagnost — as Rabelais still recalled in *Gargantua and Pantagruel*, this was the term — is ubiquitous in scenes of reading in the classical world. He reads for others; he is made to read.[3]

Some of these slaves apparently did much more than lend their voice to the text. They were real living archives, a little like in Ray Bradbury's *Fahrenheit 451*, where books that are threatened with destruction and at risk of being forgotten survive because some people have learned them by heart. This archiving role, this recording role of the reading slave, is attested in one of the open letters Seneca addresses to the young Lucilius, Roman governor of Sicily at the time of Nero's reign. He mentions a certain Calvisius Sabinius, a freed slave who seemed to be as rich as he was stupid:

> His memory was so faulty that he would sometimes forget the name of Ulysses, or Achilles, or Priam.... But none the less did he desire to appear learned. So he devised this short cut to learning: he paid fabulous prices for slaves — one to know Homer by heart and another to know Hesiod; he also

delegated a special slave to each of the nine lyric poets. . . . After collecting this retinue, he began to make life miserable for his guests; he would keep these fellows at the foot of his couch, and ask them from time to time for verses which he might repeat, and then frequently break down in the middle of a word.[4]

The anagnost was thus a sort of talking book, a precursor to Henty, a fictional character in Evelyn Waugh's short story, "The Man Who Liked Dickens." When Henty becomes the last survivor of an expedition to the Amazon, the strange Mr. McMaster takes him in and nurses him. But when he recovers, he slowly realizes that it is impossible to leave his savior's house: he is kept prisoner in order that he may read Dickens's novels out loud.

When Henty first reads to his host, who will become his jailor, he remembers that "he had always rather enjoyed reading aloud and in the first year of marriage had shared several books in this way with his wife, until one day, in one of her rare moments of confidence, she remarked that it was torture to her."[5] While being read to can thus be a source of suffering, a constraint, the subjugation clearly runs the other way at the end of this story when Henty discovers, to his horror, that he is condemned to read the same novels over and over again to the man who holds him prisoner: "Tomorrow, and the day after that, and the day after that. Let us read *Little Dorrit* again."[6]

"The Man Who Liked Dickens" gives us one account of the survival of the anagnost. But, we also continue to encounter the anagnost in ourselves when we read silently — at least this is the hypothesis I am proposing. When we open a book, it is always in some sense an anagnost who begins to read in us. The reading slave — for instance, the anonymous "boy" who is hailed, as we will see, at the beginning of Plato's *Theaetetus* — basically plays the same role as a phonograph, the contraption that Thomas Edison explicitly described as useful for reading aloud.

Books may be read by the charitably-inclined professional reader, or by such readers especially employed for that purpose, and the record of such a book used in the asylums of the blind, hospitals, the sick-chamber, or even with great profit and amusement by the lady or gentleman whose eyes and hands may be otherwise employed; or, again, because of the greater enjoyment to be had from a book when read by an elocutionist than when read by the average reader.[7]

The audiobook is a relatively recent invention (although there are visionary anticipations of it, for instance, in Cyrano de Bergerac).[8] It should, however, be considered as a continuation, like a vocal prosthesis, of reading practices that we will find staged in Plato's dialogues. And when we will observe readers beginning to read in silence, we will have to reckon with the idea that the phonography of reading (whether it be the work of the slave reading out loud or the recording on discs by professional readers) has been in some sense swallowed up, immersed in each of us, interiorized in the intimate vocal scenography that sets the stage every time we read.

There is at least one more voice that, in principle, cannot be reduced to any of those three instances (I, you, he, she, they) in the intimate phonoscene of our reading, on this triangulated stage on which *you*, the anagnost, read for *me* something that was written by someone else. This is the voice that articulates the imperative to read, the one that simply says "read!" Who enunciates this imperative? To whom does this voice belong as it issues this injunction, silently or thunderously? We will not answer this question immediately (although, by reading, we are perhaps already responding to the injunction itself). We will not immediately try to identify a "who" behind this command to read. Rather, we will let various figures appear as we read, figures who might provide incarnations of this voice, but who are also destined to pass on the role (for instance, Eucleides ordering the anagnost to read in Plato's *Theaetetus* or the mother in Sade's *Philosophy in the Bedroom*). Above all," we will respect the structural indeterminacy of this voice. It has a floating mooring, if I might put it that way, which means that it can be detached from all empirical sources to become what Kant, in the *Critique of Pure Reason*, called "the voice of reason," that "celestial" (*himmlische*) voice, this voice so clear (*so deutlich*) that a remarkable and rare adjective is required to describe it: *unüberschreibar*, in other words, literally, "impossible to drown out with cries."[9]

In short, with this supernumerary voice, we no doubt end up with a square of voices rather than a triangle.

What we should note for the moment is that like the anagnost's, the voice of the imperative is interiorized; it, too, ends up being soundless or tacit in us. Better: these two voices are perhaps interiorized at the same time, in parallel or jointly. Jesper Svenbro suggests as much in his remarkable anthropology of reading in ancient Greece: it is with "one and the same movement," he writes, that "over the course of the Vth century BC," the voice of the reader and the voice of the law came to be internalized. What he shows is that basically, the voice of the anagnost and the voice of the magistrate (or the archon) migrate inside simultaneously.[10]

I am not, however, so much interested in identifying the precise moment of the historical mutation when these two voices cross over from the external bodies in which they live into my inner conscience. I am much more interested in the possibility of the opposite journey — anachronistic, if you like — whereby what has folded into the intimate silence of reading would be unfurled in order to confront reading with the micropolitical drama that plays out in it.

"Read!": this injunction has become silent in us. I want it to echo again, through Plato and Sade's dialogues. "Take the book and read," is what we read in the prologue to the *Theaetetus*.[11] In the *Phaedrus*, it is Socrates who says to his interlocutor, "choose the position in which you think you can read most easily, and read."[12] Similarly, in the *Philosophy in the Bedroom*, the Chevalier de Mirvel obeys his sister when he reads the famous pamphlet *Français, encore un effort* (Yet another effort, Frenchmen) after she throws out "Chevalier, you possess a fine organ, read it to us."[13] However, this order that precedes and opens every act of reading can also be given in many modes other than the imperative, and, as we will see, in many forms. Thus, as an epigraph on the title page of *Philosophy in the Bedroom*, Sade inscribes a phrase whose injunctive value is in the future: "The mother will prescribe its reading to her daughter."[14]

Sometimes, the reader is given detailed directives, as when Jacques Lacan, in "Kant with Sade" (a text written as a preface to *Philosophy in the Bedroom*), interrupts after three pages to declare: "This is why we request that those of our readers who are still in a virginal relation to the *Critique of Practical Reason*, not having read it, stop at this very point of our lines, to take them up afterwards. They should check whether it indeed has the effect that we say it has."[15] At the other extreme from such specific instructions, the reading imperative can be condensed into a noun that acts like a stage direction, as is the case in Lacan's seminar, *Psychoses*, where we find a whole series of interruptions in italics: "*The reading continues*," "*Reading of the Memoirs*,"[16] and more. The noun in question (*lecture*, "reading," the French term being the same as the one on the "play" button of a tape recorder) oscillates between a constative (it indicates that here, at this moment in his seminar, Lacan read a passage from *Memoirs of my Mental Illness* by Daniel Paul Schreber) and a performative stage direction that enjoins the readers to do the same, to read in turn what is (or was) being read.

After having read this before us, just after becoming a reader under our eyes, Lacan wonders what it can mean to obey an injunction to read, whatever form it takes. More precisely, he asks what signs could attest to the order or stage direction having been executed. Indeed, addressing his audience at the time (and, beyond that, those who will one day read him), he asks, "What do you call reading? ... When are you sure that you are reading? You may say there is no doubt, that one has the feeling of reading. There are many things that go against that claim." In thus turning to us, we who were reading (and even reading him reading the *Memoirs*), Lacan gives three examples of these readings that are not really readings: first, "dreams," when we read in our dreams but in a reading that is not really one; next, "the case of someone pretending to read"; and, finally, "the case when you already know the text by heart."[17]

We need to take seriously these nonreadings that Lacan mentions, these pseudoreadings that we can witness as spectacle, that one can believe in, and that, nevertheless free themselves radically from the text. For on the one hand, when we dream that we are reading, when we pretend to read, or read what we already know by heart, we don't really read. Yet on the other hand, from these antireadings we can extrapolate the pure forms of reading, a pure reading without an object, an intransitive reading. Better: a reading that goes beyond its object, that misses it by overshooting it, as though nothing were left of the reading except its pure imperative.

"Read!" at all costs and beyond even what there is to read: what is announced, then, is a *categorical imperative* to read. Between Plato and Sade, we need to explore this.

Loving-Reading

(*Phaedrus*)

I open Plato's *Phaedrus*.

Enter Socrates and Phaedrus, as stage directions say, the latter coming from his master Lysias's house:

SOCRATES: Dear Phaedrus, wither away, and where do you come from?

PHAEDRUS: From Lysias, Socrates . . . and I am going for a walk outside the wall [of Athens].[1]

It is, thus, at the edge of the city, in the country, as we would say today, that Phaedrus tells Socrates what he heard from Lysias, his master and *erastēs*.[2]

PHAEDRUS: . . . Lysias has represented one of the beauties being tempted, but not by a lover [*erastou*]; this is just the clever thing about it; for he says that favours should be granted rather to the one who is not in love [*mē erōnti*] than to the lover.[3]

Clearly, Lysias is telling Phaedrus about the erotic relationship that a master can have with a young disciple whom he does not love, with whom he is not in love. And Socrates is dying to know more: he is determined not to let Phaedrus out of his sight; he will follow him everywhere, hound him until he agrees to *read* Lysias's speech.[4]

At the very threshold of the reading scene there thus emerges a close and complex connection between loving and reading,

47

two verbs, two gerunds, between which, for reasons that will soon become apparent, it makes sense to leave open all the possible punctuation marks, including the possibility that there be none (as though one wrote them in *scriptio continua*, with no space between them, which was a common scriptural practice in Plato's day). *Loving()reading* could then be read (or connected) at least in two different ways:

1. Lovingreading or loving-reading (a double verb, conjugated as transitive, where what one loves-reads is someone or something, Lysias or the book).
2. Loving reading (in which case, it is reading that one loves).

For Phaedrus, *loving()reading* is, above all, loving and reading, in a single verb, *someone*. Loving and reading are intertwined in this reader who loves the voice to which he listens in the text to which he lends his own body. And it is thus under the sign of this hyphen (*trait d'union*), the hyphenated loving-reading, that Plato's *Phaedrus* opens. It is as though this feature, the line contracting the space between the two verbs, some sort of silent bond where a contractual relationship between them takes place, has brought them together or joined them together in order to express the union of love and reading in the act of uniting with the one who speaks in the text.

One can indeed suppose that Phaedrus, Lysias's disciple, had already granted his master favors and is now prepared to love-read him again, for Socrates. He would have thus offered himself to Lysias without being loved in return since such seems to be the "clever" nature of the pederastic and pedagogical contract suggested in the speech that we, the readers of this dialogue, are about to hear in turn. And Socrates cannot wait to witness a sort of second playing out, a reproduction of this free union, with neither jealousy nor possession. He is burning with the desire to hear Phaedrus let himself be penetrated again by Lysias's speech or voice, by Lysias's *logos*.

Yet the actual act of reading, that act that many Greek and Latin inscriptions describe in openly sexual terms,[5] is long in coming. Phaedrus first doubts his own ability to "tell from memory" (*apomnēmoneusein*) Lysias's speech, whereas Socrates insists that he do so in a few remarkable lines, lines in which, in some sense, he splits his reticent interlocutor:

> SOCRATES: O Phaedrus! If I don't know Phaedrus, I have forgotten myself. But since neither of these things is true, I know very well that when listening to Lysias he did not hear once only [*ou monon hapax ēkousen*], but often [*pollakis*] urged him to repeat; and he gladly obeyed.[6]

It seems, then, that Lysias read his speech to Phaedrus several times; it was not a *hapax*. And in the space of this singular rejoinder, Phaedrus, who will soon read and reread it for Socrates (and thus also for we who read him), moves from the second person singular—the place of interlocution or address in a dialogue—to the third. For a moment, through these sentences addressed to *him*, rather than *you*, he appears to be absent from the scene, as though he were already taking leave or disappearing in order *to read*, that is, to lend his voice, his body, to the words of another. Before he really starts to read, before giving himself over body and soul to the one who will speak through him, Phaedrus is already no longer quite himself, is already partly another. Socrates continues, still speaking of Phaedrus to Phaedrus as though the latter were not really there: "Yet even that was not enough for Phaedrus, but at last he borrowed the book [the scroll, *to biblion*] and read what he especially wished."[7] In a sort of hyperbolic repetition, Phaedrus, one Phaedrus or the other, has thus taken hold of Lysias's writing to carry it off, to read and reread it elsewhere, outside the city walls.

What a strange manner Socrates has! What a strange way of addressing Phaedrus by splitting him in two! For when Socrates has to insist that Phaedrus actually get on with reading (Phaedrus needs to be begged), he goes literally as far as *asking Phaedrus to ask Phaedrus* to do it: "So, Phaedrus, ask him [Phaedrus] now to do what he will presently do anyway."[8] Why this insistence on addressing Phaedrus both as *you* and as *him*? It is as though Socrates already perceived, already heralded, the division that the imminent scene of reading would set up in Phaedrus, splitting him between his reading voice and the voice of the text that speaks through him.

We will constantly encounter this doubling, which, well beyond Phaedrus, constitutively affects every reader.

—☙

While Phaedrus thus divides himself, as though in preparation for reading, what excites Socrates' curiosity is the *biblion*: that's what he wants to see, the hidden object of desire that is "in your left hand, under your cloak." "Come now, show it"[9]—there is undeniable eroticism in Socrates' request, as though after having split his interlocutor, he now wanted to undress him. The attraction of the roll that carries the text of the speech, a sort of metonymy for Lysias that Phaedrus hugs, might evoke a magnificent later epigram (second century AD), one attributed to Strato:

> Fortunate little book, I am not jealous of you [meaning "would not be, even if you deserved it"]. Reading you, a boy will touch you, hold you close to his cheek or press you to his lips, or perhaps he will unfold you upon his tender thighs, O most fortunate of books! Often you will be carried within his shirt or, flung down upon a chair, you will dare to touch those particular things [*keîna*] without fear. You will speak much with him, alone with him.[10]

Once the *biblion* has thus been seen or glimpsed as an object of erotic substitution, Phaedrus and Socrates set out in search of a place where they can sit together or lie down together to read it. Plato describes the place they ultimately find, in the shade of a plane tree, as a charming place, covered in gently sloping grass. When they arrive there, Socrates and Phaedrus take up their positions or poses. Paraphrasing the stage directions we will encounter in another great text on reading and love (Sade's *Philosophy in the Bedroom*), we might say that the disposition is effected, the posture is assumed, in a way that prepares for loving-reading Lysias:

SOCRATES: So now that I have come here, I intend to lie down [*katakeises-thai*] and do you choose the position [*skhēmati*] in which you think you can read [*anagnōsesthai*] most easily, and read.

PHAEDRUS: Hear then.[11]

Lying down, Socrates lets himself be penetrated by Phaedrus's reading as Phaedrus offers himself vocally to his *erastēs* and master, Lysias. The two of them loving-reading under the plane tree is, of course, actually a threesome.

In the middle of this triangulation, it is hard to concentrate on Lysias's rather boring and poorly constructed speech, which, through Phaedrus, talks about their pedagogical and pederastic (pedcrastagogic) contract based on free love, that is to say, love without love. The long argument aims to show the *erōmenos*, who is himself reading it to a prone Socrates, that a disciple has everything to gain by giving himself over to a master who does not love him.[12]

However, we, who, like Socrates, no doubt, are more interested in Phaedrus as he reads than in what he is reading, are tempted to turn away from this arduous demonstration and toward the fascinating underlying paradox, namely, that *when Phaedrus reads*, when Phaedrus is in the middle of loving-reading his master, for those of us who read him reading, *he is not reading anymore*. I mean that in the text, when Phaedrus gets to the point of reading, there is no longer any representation of him reading. In other words, the structure of the reading point is such that it appears only as it disappears, that it manifests only intermittently, where it is interrupted, where it is being prepared or set up, where reading is going to begin or begin again.[13]

Indeed, it is when Phaedrus has *finished* reading that we *again* see him reading, that we go back to reading him as he was when he was reading (since we cannot read him reading), through the words and gaze of Socrates, who listens:

PHAEDRUS: What do you think of the discourse [*logos*], Socrates? Is it not wonderful, especially in diction?

SOCRATES: ... I am quite overcome by it. And this is due to you, Phaedrus, because as I looked at you, I saw that you were delighted by the speech as you read [*anagignōskōn*].[14]

As he is reading, Phaedrus does not only radiate Lysias's *logos*, the *logos* that penetrates him and passes through him. He also radiates the pleasure he gets from reading. As Socrates had sensed in the dialogue before the reading scene, Phaedrus splits or duplicates his reading, draws attention to it through the pleasure he takes in it, a pleasure that we can read. But for us, as we read what he reads, these marks or traces of his reading — of the activity of his reading rather than of what he reads — can be discerned only after the fact, with Socrates' retrospective comments ("while you were reading, you seemed ...").

—☙

The rest of the *Phaedrus* has been glossed so many times that I will only summarize it, pausing on what matters to us here, namely, as we will see, *rereading*.

Having undertaken to critique Lysias's speech, which he has just heard, and responding to Phaedrus's insistent request, Socrates gives a better, more inspired version of the speech under the spell of an enthusiasm that, he explains, possesses him (*enthousiasō*, 241e). Then, full of remorse when he hears his daimon's voice, Socrates launches into improvising a second speech, one that will be the exact opposite of the first, in order to correct what he now sees as sacrilegious or impious with respect to the god of Love (*Erōs*): "I am afraid of Love himself," he explains to Phaedrus, and so he "wish[es] to wash out the brine from [his] ears with the water of a sweet discourse."[15]

Through this speech washing (one *logos* wiping out another), Socrates inaugurates a general movement of inversion in the dialogue that will become a hymn to the *mania* of love and all its positive effects on the soul. Phaedrus, the *erōmenos*, finds himself in a novel role facing his *erastēs*, Lysias. As Sade would say, the posture is dissolved, the attitudes are dissolved,[16] and in the ensuing permutation, Phaedrus is given an unexpected place in the loving-reading scene: "PHAEDRUS: . . . When you have spoken the praise of the lover, Lysias must of course be compelled by me to write another discourse on the same subject."[17]

Everything gets turned around here, as though Phaedrus, who now promises to dictate his future speeches to Lysias, had become the latter's *erastēs* while becoming henceforth *erōmenos* to Socrates, his *erastēs*. There is a circulating revolution in this threesome that carries them to loving-reading each other backward or upside down.

Socrates once again addresses Phaedrus in the third person, but this time as a love object, the object of a love contract that Phaedrus seems to countersign similarly through an oblique pronouncement, speaking of himself as of another:

> SOCRATES: Where is the youth [*pais*] to whom I was speaking? He must hear this also, lest if he do not hear it, he accept a non-lover [*tō mē erōnti*]. . . .
> PHAEDRUS: Here he is, always close at hand, whenever you want him.[18]

But why, on the threshold of the big speech Socrates is about to improvise to celebrate the delirium brought on by love — this *mania* that, as he will put it, is the anamnesis of true beauty, when souls recover memories of contemplating essence and truth (*ousia* and *alētheia*, 247c–d), glimpsed as they reach the end of their journey on the outer surface of the heavens — why does Socrates again make use of this strange way of addressing his interlocutor as though he were both present and absent, both here and elsewhere, both himself and another?

You may have guessed that my hypothesis is that Phaedrus, both as a reader and then as the auditor of another's speech (Lysias's and now Socrates'), is indeed double, divided: as he prepares to read or to listen, Phaedrus splits into the *erōmenos* (the passive Phaedrus who makes himself into a pure transparent vehicle for the voice that speaks through him) and the *erastēs* (the Phaedrus who reads or listens to that voice, in the most active senses of those verbs). And it is precisely because there are two Phaedruses, so to speak, because one Phaedrus hides another, that the permutation, the cycling revolution of loving-reading can take place, one Phaedrus taking over from the other.

I would like to take this one step further: the doubling that Plato stages as though it were the precondition of any reading (as I read, I split into my reading voice and the voice that I read), this division is intrinsically — albeit subterraneously — connected to what is perhaps the most quietly remarkable event of this dialogue, namely, that Socrates soon asks Phaedrus to *reread* Lysias's speech. He actually suggests rereading several times, only to observe in the end, together, that they do not like this *logos*, the dry, rather weak speech that advocates not loving.

Both of these rereadings take place after Socrates holds forth for the second time, when the dialogue is moving toward a debate no longer about beauty in general, or beauty in love, but about the beauty of speeches, a beauty that also supposes knowledge of truth. Lysias's speech is first evaluated according to this criterion:

> SOCRATES: Then, my friend, he who knows not the truth [*tēn alētheian*], but pursues opinions, will, it seems, attain an art of speech [*logōn technēn*] which is ridiculous, and not an art at all [*atekhnon*].
>
> PHAEDRUS: Probably.
>
> SOCRATES: Shall we look in the speech of Lysias, which you have with you, and in what I said, for something which we think shows art [*entechnōn*] and the lack of art?... Read me the beginning of Lysias' discourse [*anagnōthi tēn tou Lusiou logou archēn*].[19]

Phaedrus obliges, rereading the lines we have already read with him. However, as though once were not enough, as though it were necessary that a rereading, like a reading, not remain a *hapax* (to use the term that you will remember Socrates uses at the very beginning of the dialogue), Phaedrus will have to *reread again*, reread a second time: "SOCRATES: Read [*lege*], that I may hear Lysias himself."[20]

Rereading here is not at all passive. The passivity of reading flips into an active rereading, given that, as it is reread, Lysias's speech is judged, analyzed, criticized, that is it is also disassembled, decomposed, dismembered into its constituent parts:

> SOCRATES: He [Lysias] certainly does not at all seem to do what we demand, for he does not even begin at the beginning [*ap' archēs*], but undertakes to swim on his back up the current of his discourse from its end [*apo teleutēs*].[21]

Indeed, contrary to Socrates, Lysias did not proceed in an orderly fashion, defining love at the beginning. That is why, being upside down, his speech does not follow the rule that would take the beauty or the harmony of the body as a model:

> SOCRATES: . . . Every discourse must be organized, like a living being [*ōsper zōon*], with a body [*sōma*] of its own, as it were, so as not to be headless [*akephalon*] nor footless [*apoun*].[22]

Diagnosing what now seems to them to be a clumsy inversion of the organic parts of the speech, Socrates and Phaedrus turn around, or upside down, the erotics of power in loving-reading. In other words, as their critical judgment spins the speech around, the corporal postures of the reading scene are also rearranging themselves. Lysias, whom Phaedrus could already imagine — as Socrates was about to begin his second speech[23] — being *forced* to write under his dictation, now is clearly in the position of the one *suffering* the reading. In other words, and to put it crudely (that is, in the terms of many Greek and Latin inscription or epigrams, such as the one attributed to Strato), whereas during the first reading, Lysias was penetrating Phaedrus, who was penetrating Socrates, this time Socrates penetrates Phaedrus, who penetrates Lysias.

Rereading thus foreshadows the possibility of reshuffling the roles: not only the members of the discursive organism, the parts and articulations of the *corpus* of the text that is read, but also, above all, the bodies of those who read and the relationships of domination in which they are caught are rearranged. This is the chance for a change, an exchange of positions or a swapping of partners in the pederastic psychagogy of reading.[24]

It is, of course, an open question what remains of the Phaedrus, Socrates, Lysias threesome, what happens to their switching triangle, when reading goes silent. Might it be that they resurface in us every time we read? Might it be that we carry them in us, throughout the subvocalizing mumbling that is tacitly active in our inner selves as readers?

The Nameless Reader

(*Theaetetus*)

We know the name of the one who reads and rereads Lysias's speech for Socrates: it is Phaedrus. In the *Theaetetus*, a later dialogue (in it, we learn that Socrates is dead), we know nothing about the one who, like Phaedrus, reads both diegetically (he reads in the story that is told, he reads for the other characters) and metadiegetically (he reads also, as it were, jumping out of the story, since he reads for us who read through him). Whereas Phaedrus partially disappeared when he began to read (it was only after the fact that we read about him reading, and his was only a partial disappearance since he resurfaced when he resumed his dialogue with Socrates), in the *Theaetetus*, the one in whom we are interested this time disappears completely. Contrary to Phaedrus, he totally disappears. *Or almost*, otherwise how would we even know he had disappeared?

In a way, our reading of the *Theaetetus* will try to do justice to this anonymous reader. We may not be able to recover his name, but we will at least try to restore him to the place that is rightfully his. We will put him back in the role that was stolen from him; we will cite him in the credits.

But wait, you may say, is this still reading, if we are adding a character to the dramatis personae of a Platonic dialogue? Wouldn't that instead be a rewriting of the dialogue? Of course, I could retort that reading is always rewriting in a way insofar as it involves marking, remarking, annotating, correcting, glossing. . . . But let me reassure you: no, we will not add anything or anyone to the *Theaetetus*. We will scrupulously and faithfully stick to the text as it is in itself. For by reintroducing the reader who has been repressed out of the scene, we will in fact simply underline the mute — is it really mute? — presence of the one who was *already there*. Already there, however, without being so, present-absent, without his own voice, without his name (or even his role) being credited.

The one whose appearance, or reappearance in the *Theaetetus* we are about to allow is the slave reader, the anagnost. He reads for those who listen. And he does not speak in his own name — the proper name he does not have — since he only lends his voice to the characters to whom he gives life by reading.[1] He does not actually participate in the dialogue, he does not have the status to address Socrates directly, however briefly. Thus, he does not enunciate anything. He is the addressee of a single apostrophe, and his only answer is to obey. This is toward the end of the prologue between Terpsion and Eucleides. And it is the latter who, having mentioned him once in the third person — "Come, let us go, and while we are resting, the boy shall read to us" — addresses him: "Come, boy [*pai*], take the book [*labe to biblion*] and read [*kai lege*]."[2]

The anonymous anagnost does not answer anything to this reading imperative; he simply obeys mutely. Or one could say exactly the opposite since he gives the longest possible answer: by obeying, by reading the dialogue that follows this prologue, he will not stop talking. And he who has no voice, he whose status as a slave condemns him to silence, takes on all the voices; he is the archspeaker, the hypertalker, who sounds them each out in turn.

How, then, does the anagnost, who acts as a sort of telephone switchboard or sound engineer, organize the casting of voices?

Eucleides explains this in the prologue before the imperative ("read!") to the slave. Indeed, there, Euclides tells of transcribing on a notebook (*biblion*) what Socrates told him of his conversations with Theaetetus and Theodorus:

EUCLEIDES: When I went to Athens he [Socrates] related [*diēgēsato*] to me the conversation [*logous*] he had with him, which was well worth hearing. . . .

TERPSION· But what was the talk [*logoi*]? Could you relate it [*diēgēsasthai*]?

EUCLEIDES: No, by Zeus, at least not offhand. But I made notes at the time as soon as I reached home, then afterwards at my leisure, as I recalled things, I wrote them down, and whenever I went to Athens, I used to ask Socrates about what I could not remember, and then I came here and made corrections; so that I have pretty much the whole talk written down.[3]

Strictly speaking, the dialogue we are about to read between Socrates, Theodorus, and Theaetetus is thus entirely written down by Eucleides who, before disappearing with Terpsion at the end of this prologue, carefully explains how these notes (*hupomnēmata*) were assembled:

EUCLEIDES: Here is the book [*biblion*], Terpsion. Now this is the way I wrote the conversation [*ton logon*]: I did not represent Socrates relating it to me, as he did [*ouk emoi Sōkratō dēgoumenon hōs diēgeito*], but conversing with those with whom he told me he conversed [*alla dialegomenon hois ephē dialechthēnai*]. And he told me they were the geometrician Theodorus and Theaetetus.[4]

The injunction to read ("read!"), this order that marks the end of the prologue a few lines later, thus comes to punctuate the erasure of Socrates' indirect style: instead of relating the conversation, Socrates can move to a direct style, conversing with his interlocutors. It is as though the anagnost's fleeting appearance between the prologue and the dialogue were connected to Socrates' disappearance in his role as a narrator, the better to make room for the Socrates who is involved in a direct dialogue, "conversing with those with whom . . . he conversed."[5] For at least one can say, for the moment, that the anagnost appears precisely where Eucleides is trying to avoid what might "be annoying in the written account, such as 'and I said' or 'and I remarked,' whenever Socrates spoke, or 'he agreed' or 'he did not agree,' in the case of the interlocutor."[6]

59

Thus, the anagnost appears-disappears — he shows up without saying anything, although henceforth he will say everything that is said — at the very moment when the issue is what needs to be repressed in order to make space in the scene of the dialogue for the characters of Socrates, Theodorus, and Theaetetus *as they are in themselves.* (Plato has this beautiful expression, *auton autois,* "himself with themselves," to describe the way Socrates and his interlocutors speak directly, without a narrative intermediary.) The anagnost, who is barely evoked before falling back into apparent oblivion, takes on all the formulas that signal the indirect discourse that threatens the identity of the voices in the dialogue; he takes them with him into the shadows to which he withdraws.

The slave reader is thus *destined* to be forgotten, precisely so that the direct style can shine forth in its immediacy. And indeed, he generally does get forgotten in most of the commentaries that have been written about this late Platonic dialogue. In his vast and fascinating classification of the types of "narrative metalepsis" (the passage or leap from one narrative level to another), Gérard Genette considers the *Theaetetus*'s prologue as the "archetype" of this type, which he calls the "reduced metadiegetic,"[7] the fact of *recounting* how the metadiegetic narrator (in this case, Eucleides describing to Terpsion the way he took notes) is effaced in favor of a simple diegetic regime (Socrates, Theodorus, and Theaetetus in direct dialogue).

He does not, however, say a word about the anagnost, who is, as we have seen, the one who operates this reduction or this flattening, since by lending his anonymous voice, he is the one who makes it possible to declutter the diegesis. Referring to Genette's analysis, Jean-François Lyotard, in *The Differend*, goes even further in a forgetting that looks awfully like a repression. It is worth examining this passage, which does not mention the anagnost, because having repeated the narrative congestion of the prologue, Lyotard makes the slave reader figure disappear, as though by magic, *at the very moment where he insists on the readers that we are*:

> He [Genette] sees the archetype of metalepsis in the preamble to the *The-aetetus*. Euclides reports to Terpsion a debate between Theaetetus, Theodorus, and Socrates, reported to him by Socrates himself. In order, though, to avoid the tedious repetition of narrative markings such as *he said*, *he answered*, *I said*, or *he agreed*, Euclides, who wrote down the conversation from memory, suppressed such formulas from the book. Terpsion and we, Euclides' readers, therefore read Socrates' dialogue with Theaetetus and Theordorus as if he (Terpsion) and we were listening to them with no intermediary informant. This is a case of perfect mimesis: recognizable by the writer's effacement, by Euclides' apocryptism.[8]

The dissimulation (what Lyotard calls the apocryptism, from the Greek *apokruptein*, to hide, to cover), the erasure of the scriptor (Eucleides), masks and perfects at the same time: it masks and accomplishes the obliteration of the reader (the anagnost). We have here the erasure of his very erasure: his *almost* total eclipse in Plato's dialogue is thus *completed*.

Perhaps the most striking thing here is that Lyotard, when he then objects that the mimetic transparency of Platonic dialogues is often rendered opaque by the "proliferation of the levels" of narration in the prologues, concludes from that that we, the readers, are "thrown at a distance by the stage-setting operations" and that "our identification with the partners in the dialogue seems delayed."[9] What Lyotard does not say is that this imperfect or delayed identification takes place against the backdrop of an identification that is so perfect that it erases itself, making way for the most immediate identity. Because *we are* the anagnost. Or rather, and more precisely, it is a part of us, it is the voice that, tacit or almost silent, subvocal, whispers the text in us, even as it constantly withdraws. When we read, we all carry an anagnost within.

As his voice becomes interiorized over the following centuries, the slave reader will disappear from the scene, taking with him the trace of the violence — of the domination — to which he was subjected. However, as it is buried, this violence is not simply neutralized, and my hypothesis is that reading remains determined throughout by power relations that are constantly redistributed within the reader.

In the *Theaetetus*, Plato seems to anticipate, by staging it, the way we as readers absorb the anagnost. And we become incapable of reading this reading slave reading, even as, henceforth, we carry him within ourselves. Indeed, contrary to what happens in the *Phaedrus*, here, we will see or hear nothing about how the anagnost reads what he reads, namely, the dialogue that we read with and through him. For good reason: given that his reading is coextensive with ours, *for us* he never stops reading, he never starts again or rereads, never comments on his reading, and no other character ever notes anything about him (as Socrates did when he marveled at the way Phaedrus exuded happiness while reading). If the *Theaetetus* is a scene of reading, it is one that is not limited to a specific moment in the dialogue (like Phaedrus reading to Socrates in the shade of a plane tree). It is rather one single great reading scene that can almost not be distinguished from the dialogue as a whole, even as it is paradoxically pushed off the scene into the half-erased backstage of a prologue. The *Theaetetus*, precisely because it is a dialogue that *is read from beginning to end before we even read it*, reveals its reading only reluctantly, in the fold or the one open chink of its layered narrative. Basically, the only thing that one can say about the disappearing reading by the anagnost in the *Theaetetus* is that it continues to disappear or that it disappears in order to continue, that it continuously disappears, that it is nothing but a continuing and continued disappearance making way for the transparency of our own reading.

—☙

Is that the last word? Is there really nothing left of the anagnost once he has read for us? Does nothing of him persist, is nothing visible, is there nothing that might be noticed at the surface of the diegesis that he carries underground?

Before we leave these scenes of Platonic reading full of anag-nosts, *erastai*, and *orōmenoi* to turn to the more complex, and more violent, scenes in Sade, allow me two remarks.

1. There is a singular, almost fantastical (*unheimlich*) passage where the dialogue between Socrates, Theodorus, and Theaete-tus appears to them almost to be a dream. Socrates, contesting the Theaetetus's proposed definition of knowledge as "sensation" (*aisthēsis*), tests the definition by referring to the "controversy" (*amphisbētēma*) that it might provoke:

> SOCRATES: ... What proof you could give if anyone should ask us now, at the present moment, whether we are asleep and our thoughts are a dream, or whether we are awake and talking with each other in a waking condition?
> THEAETETUS: Really, Socrates, I don't see what proof can be given.... Take, for instance, the conversation we have just had: there is nothing to prevent us from imagining in our sleep also that we are carrying on this con-versation with each other [*en tōi hupnōi dokein allēlois dialegesthai*], and when in a dream we imagine that we are relating dreams [*onar oneirata dokōmen diēgeisthai*], the likeness between the one talk and the other is remarkable [*atopos hē homoiotēs toutōn ekeinois*].[10]

Theaetetus suggests that his dialogue with Socrates could be a fiction. And when his character thus imagines himself, for a moment, as though he saw himself from the outside, as though he were observing the dialogue from the vantage point of the pro-logue, we are almost dealing with one of those narrative metalepses that Genette describes as an "intrusion ... by diegetic characters into a metadiegetic universe."[11] Could it be that Theaetetus here remembers, in an obscure and displaced way, his own status as a character *being read*?

2. We cannot fail to be struck by what seems to be a return, also displaced, of the anagnost and his reading at the moment of the final failure that will leave the dialogue bereft of any satisfying

conclusion. The *Theaetetus* indeed ends, or stops, or is interrupted, with a moment of disillusion: Socrates declares to Theaetetus that all that is left of their exchanges is just "hot air" (*anemiaia*).[12]

Shortly before this dead-end epilogue, however, there has been another attempt at defining knowledge as "true opinion accompanied by reason" (*doxan alēthē meta logou*).[13] And Socrates tests this definition through extended recourse to the analogy with syllabic reading:

> SOCRATES: the syllables have a rational explanation [*sullabai logon echousi*], but the letters [*stoicheia*] have not [*aloga*, that is without reason, without *logos*]? ... Now if anyone should ask about the first syllable of Socrates; "Theaetetus, tell me, what is SO?" What would you reply?
>
> THEAETETUS: I should say "S and O."
>
> SOCRATES: This, then, is your explanation [*logon*] of the syllable?
>
> THEAETETUS: Yes.
>
> SOCRATES: Come now, in the same manner give me an explanation of the S [*ton tou sigma logon*].
>
> THEAETETUS: How can one give any elements of an element [*kai pōs tou stoicheiou tis erei stoicheia*]?[14]

The rest of the argument, leading to the final fatal interruption, boils down to saying that if one cannot give the reason for the elements, which are in turn the reason for the syllables they compose, then it is equally impossible to define knowledge of their composite sum as a true opinion accompanied by reason.

It is striking to see that just before the failure that will mark the end of their dialogue, Socrates and Theaetetus find themselves miming a pure and simple reading, with no reason: they spell out words the way one deciphers a text that one cannot get into, as though, without knowing it or wanting to, they were playing the part of that kind of reading machine that is an anagnost. The latter, while letting himself be forgotten in the interiorization that makes him disappear in us, seems to want to reappear at the surface. It is as though we heard muffled thumping from backstage, a certain someone reminding us of his existence.

The Categorical Imperative of Reading

(*Philosophy in the Bedroom*)

After listening to the triangulated reading scene — Phaedrus reads Lysias for Socrates, the nameless anagnost reads Socrates or Theodorus or Theaetetus for Eucleides or Terpsion — after examining the circulations and permutations in the three-way scenes of loving-reading or requesting reading, we must now turn to the categorical imperative ("read!") that is added to the triangle. Or perhaps that subtends the triangle, determining its angles.

This imperative was certainly not absent from the reading moments we have just observed: in the *Phaedrus*, it is Socrates who voices it ("read," he says to Phaedrus); in the *Theaetetus*, it was Eucleides ("take the book and read," he said to the anagnost). In both cases, however, the imperative was thus included in or collapsed into the position of the addressee of the reading, the one who listens to the reading. In other words, the imperative did not have its own place in the triangulated reading scene. It was absorbed and, so to speak, obfuscated by what we might call addressedness of the reading that it seemed to serve.

It is time to take measure of this imperative's force and autonomy. Even if it can in fact be enunciated by the person to whom the reading will be addressed, it remains in principle independent of this position; it cannot be reduced to this position. The one who gives the order to read is not necessarily the one for whom the reading is performed.

Our triangle or threesome is thus about to be expanded into a square, a foursome. And through this quadrangular expansion, our theory of reading — our *anagnosology*, to use Roland Barthes's expression[1] — is about to acknowledge and make appropriate room for what can be described as a categorical imperative. This is an imperative that must be obeyed for no reason, without calculation, without interest, without conditions ("categorical" as opposed to "hypothetical," following the distinction Kant first drew in his *Foundations of the Metaphysics of Morals* before taking it up again in the *Critique of Pure Reason* three years later).

As far as the scene of reading and the micropolitics that play out there are concerned, the categorical imperative that I postulate sounds something like this: read whatever happens, read for the sake of reading, read no matter what you read, despite what you read, even if, or precisely because, it is unreadable. In other words, read unconditionally, without anything, without any benefit that might justify or determine your reading — read absolutely![2]

What better to test such an injunction than Sade's work, with its innumerable passages that are unreadable because they are unbearable? The first time I read the last pages of *Philosophy in the Bedroom*, those unbearable pages in which the mother is sewn up (we will try to look at them as closely as possible), I had to keep reading with my hand in front of my eyes — that is what I do when I force myself to watch horror movies — spreading my fingers slightly, as though I hoped thereby to filter what reaches me from the text, distilling atrocities, measuring them out one drop at a time, in order to be able to endure them. And why? What pushed me to read nevertheless? What dictate was I responding to in pursuing my reading whatever the conditions, whatever the object? Was I, like the characters in Sade's book, also obeying an inflexible command?

Sade forces us as readers to experience *as we read* the unconditional and absolute obedience required by the categorical imperative. At the same time, he also stages this obedience, according to another version of the loving-reading we first glimpsed with the classical *erastēs* and *erōmenos.* The Sadian scenes that await us will thus also be, as in Plato, scenes in which power and love cannot be separated (love without love, Lysias style). These scenes will induce us to think that when it is a matter of reading, when reading is at stake, *erōs* and *kratos* are always participants. Here, then, are erotocratic scenes.

Finally, as we have had a first inkling, the Kantian categorical imperative, as well as the Sadian version (to which we will return with Lacan), is also a voice that, like that of the *lectio tacita* to which Isidore de Seville referred, is an infravoice, a hypophonic voice. Granted, when Kant speaks of the "voice of reason," he says it is so powerful that it is "impossible to cover with cries" (that is how I suggest we translate *unüberschreibar*, that singular adjective we had already encountered in the *Critique of Practical Reason*). However powerfully it may boom, this voice remains an inner voice, a voice from within, a voice no one hears except the one who, as Kant puts it, tries in vain to defend himself in his own eyes without managing in the slightest to "reduce to silence the prosecutor within" (*den Ankläger in ihm keineswegs zum Verstummen bringen könne*).[3]

So far, we have been considering a phonic triangle featuring the anagnost (or his modern equivalents) when he reads what someone else has written and addresses his reading to me, to me who listens, while occasionally apostrophizing him; this is the vocal trio that plays out silently in me each time. The reading imperative introduces a fourth voice into this trio. Let us try to sound out its multiple connections to the three others. It blends in with their texture in ways that are both resounding and inaudible, vociferating and subvocal. It can sometimes be distinguished, but often it gets lost, merging into the others.

Philosophy in the Bedroom has two reading scenes.

The first, in the "Fifth Dialogue," is sparked by Eugénie's question: "I should like to know whether manners are truly necessary in a governed society."⁴ This leads to an exchange between Dolmancé and Madame de Saint-Ange:

> DOLMANCÉ: Why, by God, I have something here with me. As I left home this morning I bought . . . a little pamphlet, which if one can believe the title, ought surely to answer your question. . . . It's come straight from the press.
> MADAME DE SAINT-ANGE: Let me see it. (*She reads*:) "Yet Another Effort, Frenchmen, If You Would Become Republicans." Upon my word, 'tis an unusual title: 'tis promising; Chevalier, you possess a fine organ, read it to us. . . .
> LE CHEVALIER: Well, I'll begin.⁵

It is of course impossible to decide which organ is being referred to: is it the vocal organ necessary for reading the pamphlet, or the other one, the sexual one, which has just been amply shown and demonstrated?

This reading scene includes, to be more precise, two *reading points* like those we came across in the *Phaedrus* and the *Theaetetus*: first, this starting point, which we just read, and second, the end, almost a hundred pages further on in the first edition.⁶ It is Eugénie who punctuates the end of the reading of the pamphlet by saying to Dolmancé: "Now, it strikes me as a very solidly composed document."⁷ As we saw in Plato, reading as it takes place is destined only to appear through its punctuation after the fact. Like the slave in the *Theaetetus*, the reading the Chevalier had to disappear in order that we could read the pamphlet through him. And that is no doubt why, after he stops reading, he requests permission to "cast a glance" on the "Principles of Dolmancé" and "try to annihilate them,"⁸ principles that are so close to those of the pamphlet that Eugénie just admitted being tempted to believe Dolmancé wrote it. After having been the pamphlet's author's *erōmenos*, the Chevalier would like somehow to reread it in order to become his *erastēs*, to permute the reading positions, to rearrange the postures we could say, using Sade's lexicon.

The second reading scene is also placed under the sign of repetition and permutation since the same text, a letter from Eugenie's father, is read twice, by two different characters fifty pages apart.[9] The missive is first read by Madame de Saint-Ange to Eugénie, who is afraid of provoking her father's anger or a paternal interdiction, whereas in fact, the father, by warning of her mother's imminent arrival, is only protecting his daughter's initiation to libertinage:

EUGÉNIE: My father!... then we are lost!...

MADAME DE SAINT-ANGE: Let's read it before we get upset. (*She reads*:) "Would you believe it, my dear lady? My unbearable wife, alarmed by my daughter's journey to your house, is leaving immediately, with the intention of bringing Eugénie home. She imagines all sorts of things... which, even were one to suppose them real, would, in truth, be but very ordinary and human indeed. I request you to punish her impertinence with exceeding rigor."[10]

This letter from the father prescribing punishment for the mother — she will be sewn, according to what Barthes considered to be the most "disturbing" of "the tortures Sade imagines"[11] — this letter, then, which precedes and announces the mother ("she will arrive shortly after my letter; keep yourself in readiness,"[12] warns the father), will be reread but punctuated by a reading point that is more intermittent and evanescent than ever. It is at the very end of the book, as Dolmancé concludes the seventh and last dialogue. It appears as a stage direction in parenthesis and in italics, which leaves us, readers, furtively imagining the presence of the said letter, as though it were for a moment under our eyes:

DOLMANCÉ: And now all's been said. (*To Madame de Mistival*:) Hey! Whore, you may clothe yourself and leave when you wish. I must tell you that your husband authorized the doing of all that has just been done to you. We told you as much; you did not believe it (*He shows her the letter.*) May this example serve to remind you that your daughter is old enough to do what she pleases.... Get out; the Chevalier will escort you home. Salute the company, whore! On your knees, bow down before your daughter, and beseech her pardon for your abominable use of her.... You, Eugénie, bestow two good smacks upon Madame your Mother and as soon as she gains the threshold, help her cross it with a few lusty kicks aimed at her ass. (*All this is done.*) Farewell, Chevalier; don't fuck Madame on the highway: remember she is sewn up.[13]

One might then say that *Philosophy in the Bedroom* closes, like the mother, on this repetition of a prior reading that was also, as we will see, connected to sewing.

However, *first*, remember that the mother is the metonymy for nothing less than the injunction, the reading imperative that opens *Philosophy in the Bedroom*. Granted, there are plenty of mothers in the text: Eugénie's mother, whose cruel punishment we have just witnessed, this mother she "hates" and that Madame de Saint-Ange describes as "superstitious, pious, a shrew, a scold . . . with her revolting prudery"[14] — what Dolmancé calls "nature, mother to us all"[15] — the nation as a mother, referred to in the pamphlet when the author speaks of "a republic where every individual must have no other dam than the nation."[16] However, before this or that particular or general mother, there is the mother who makes it possible for them to appear in the reading, the mother from the prescriptive epigraph (the one who, as we read, "prescribes the reading"): there is this arch mother, who comes before all the readable mothers, from the threshold prior to the book, from the foremost edge of the text she opens up.

Second, sewing is never far from being a figure for reading (*legere* in Latin not only means to pick up, to bind, like *legein* in Greek, but also to curl up, as in rolling up a ball of wool). In *Aline and Valcour*, the epistolary novel that Sade finally managed to have printed the same year as *Philosophy in the Bedroom*, Monsieur Delcour's only concern about Sophie's education is that she learn to "read, write, sew" ("sewing — sewing and reading . . . is all a girl needs").[17]

It is, however, above all in Lacan that we have the clearest indication of the tightly bound solidarity between reading and sewing: the drawn-out metaphor of the quilting stitch offers a very precise description of the movement of Lacan's reading of the first scene of Jean Racine's *Athalie*. Here, for him, reading becomes a matter of punctuation or better, of the puncture of stitching, in other words the entering and exiting of the "upholsterer's needle," which binds the signifier and the signified together, thus ensuring the seam of signification.[18]

Reading the unbearable, terrible final scene of *Philosophy in the Bedroom* in which the mother is sewn up—I will quote only a few carefully selected points—we see literally a superposition, as though a superimpression, of sewing as pricking (*piqûre*) and punctuation as reading. Indeed, as the libertines let loose and prick ever more with the help of "a large needle with a big red waxed thread" (at the height of excitement, Dolmancé even ends up doing nothing else than "multiply his pricking"), we find punctuation in the form of ellipses (*points de suspension*), those three dots that punctuate the scene so insistently. When Dolmancé enjoins Eugénie to "multiply your stiches, so that the seam will be quite solid," she replies, "I'll take, if necessary, over two hundred of them...."[19] In the original version of 1795, Sade added four dots as punctuation marks. Or again, when blinded by pleasure and desire, and she cries out, "I can see no longer, my stiches go everywhere," she immediately adds "Look at it! Do you see how my needles wanders..." (three dots), "to her thighs, her tits...." (four dots).

Let us for the moment put it this way: if, on the one hand, the mother is the other name for the reading imperative, and on the other hand, reading is figured as sewing, then the sewn mother must have something to teach us about how that imperative is tacked (*faufilé*) into the text.[20]

Let us now try to take one further step into this matter of tacking, or sewing-reading, following Lacan as he, in turn, reads the grueling last pages of *Philosophy in the Bedroom.*

Lacan does not focus directly on the reading imperative whose stitching (*piqués*) in the texture of the text I have highlighted. He looks instead and more generally at what becomes of the Kantian imperative in Sade's version, which is just as intransigent, just as unconditional. Sade's law of *jouissance* at all cost is as absolute a prescription as Kant's moral law. That is why Lacan can see in Sade's "vindication of the crime" an "indirect avowal of the Law."[21]

Lacan finds the example par excellence of this secret correspondence between the Kantian and Sadian imperatives in the scene in which the mother is sewn, the final scene of the book and the scene with which Lacan closes his own attempt at a preface. Indeed, in the conclusion of "Kant with Sade," Lacan says that Dolmancé is "someone whom the ordinary [genital] path seems to frighten more than is fitting, and who—did Sade see it?—closes the affair with a *Noli tangere matrem*," that is to say with the stitching that prohibits touching the mother, penetrating her, or "fucking her," as the libertines say. Of this banned mother who has been withdrawn from any exchange of pleasure or *jouissance*, Lacan says: "V...ed and sewn up, the mother remains forbidden. Our verdict on the submission of Sade to the Law is confirmed."[22]

Before we even try to guess what is hidden by that word with a hole ("V...ed"), the first thing we can say—it stands out immediately—is that Lacan, the great thinker of *piqué* in reading, adds more dots and punctuation to the stitches (*piqûres*) that already pierce Sade's text. Why this V with a space and three dots? Why these marks, which we know as marks of censorship in texts that must conform to seemliness? Why the ellipsis that seems to empty the V word (or avoid it since thereby nothing is said as to what word it is) at the very same moment as it sews it up, at the same time as it punctuates it and spells it out silently?

Noli tangere matrem, says Lacan: do not touch the mother, of course. However, since mother is the other name for it, we must also immediately add: do not touch the reading (prescription), *noli tangere lectionem*. Sewing not only forbids the mother as sexual object, it also forbids the mother as a reading imperative (the one who "prescribes the reading," as the title page of the *Philosophy* put it).[23] This is what is inaccessible, out of reach, as the very law that dictates that the text be read, whatever happens and come what may, categorically, unconditionally.[24] This law thus remains and must remain *hors texte* or outside the work, preserved in an epigraph while reinscribed, sewn back into the texture of the text itself, again and again, by these dotted stitches through which the reading voice passes in and out in such a way as to appear and disappear according the intermittent anagnosological rhythm that is the very structure of its *reading points.*

"V...ed": with this word made of dot stitches, Lacan summarizes and condenses the moments in the final scene of *Philosophy* in which the unleashed cruel *jouissance* (the suture torture) seems to go beyond language, spilling over into the unsayable of an ellipsis. However, although this signifier is unreadable — it cannot be spelled or sounded out (the letters are missing) — Lacan nevertheless gives us this word to read. Is it not, in fact, precisely where the text becomes incomplete, where reading cannot grasp it, that reading goes after the text most insistently? Is it not precisely when the text is riddled with dots that we experience an absolute wanting to read (*vouloir-lire*)?

The categorical imperative to read is only such, that is to say categorical, in prescribing reading beyond the text in the text, reading the gaps and the absences. And this is no doubt why readers of Lacan reading Sade are so intent on deciphering the sutured word, the "V...ed" pierced by a space and three dot stiches. They cannot help trying to fill in the holes, sound out the gaps. Some read "raped" (*violée*), some "veiled" (*voilée*), others "syphilized" (*vérolée*).[25] Without contesting any of these three possibilities, I would like to add another that seems inescapable, given our focus: "voiced (*voisée*)."

Why do I insist on making this hollowed-out word into the signifier for voicing, that is, in terms of the structural phonology in which Lacan was steeped, what characterizes a consonant pronounced in such a way that the vocal chords vibrate (compare *zzzz* and *ssss* while touching your throat)? Why thus inscribe the voice exactly where it seems to have withdrawn in the silence of mute punctuation?

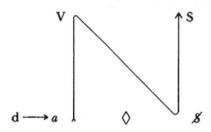

The letter V cannot fail to evoke the same letter as it figures in the well-known, but eminently enigmatic schema or graph with which Lacan formalizes what he calls "the Sadian fantasy."[26] Of course, nothing in what Lacan or his commentators say about this graph indicates that it is about voice.[27] The "V" is first and foremost the initial for what Lacan calls the "will to *jouissance*" (*volonté de jouissance*). And the graph shows that in line with the movement of desire (d), the Sadian subject projects itself as the instrument of that will—as serving its cause, what Lacan here calls object *a*—aiming, through an infinite suffering inflicted on its victim, at a pure passion (*pâtir*), a state of undivided plenitude that would fantasmatically reconstruct a raw or full subject (S), a subject not yet (or no longer) divided by the Law's bar (Ŝ). Lacan says that it is precisely "at the cost of being merely the instrument of *jouissance*"—as serving a supreme cause to which it submits unconditionally—that the Sadian subject can aim at "the reconstructed subject of alienation," that is to say, the subject recomposing its lost totality.

However, from a number of indications given by Lacan himself, we might also infer that the V in the graph could refer to "voice" or to the distribution of voices that is at stake in reading. Indeed, when Lacan talks about the law in Kant and in Sade, he says that "the good which is the object of the moral law . . . is indicated to us by our experience of *listening within ourselves to commandments,* whose imperative presents itself as categorical, that is, unconditional."[28] Or, this time about the Sadian maxim that just as unconditionally proclaims the right of enjoyment over another's body, "the herald of the maxim does not need to be anything more than a point of emission,"[29] as though it could be reduced to "a voice on the radio" that has become the "voice of conscience."[30] The V of the graph, reinscribed as the first letter of the half word "V . . . ed," is thus also that of the imperative voice, the voice of the will dictating.

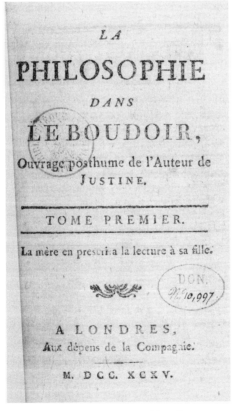

Title page of the first edition of
La Philosophie dans le Boudoir (London, 1795)

As we saw, for the reader, this imperative, which demands unconditional obedience, is embodied by the mother outside the text, through her absolute and untouchable prescription ("The mother will prescribe its reading to her daughter.") And it is by projecting himself at the service of this voice (whose vocality or vociferation, like that of Kant's moral law, can be tacit or quiet) that the reader aims at a pure, uninterrupted reading: the anagnost's reading, a sort of reading machine the way the Sadian victims are suffering machines, a fantasy of a reader's body that would simply suffer, without any caesura from the voice of the listening other.

Yet V is also exactly where the voice divides itself between two diverging branches (<), which lead to two paths or journeys:[31] on the one hand, there is the voice of the continuously reading anagnost, a full, smooth voice that lends itself infinitely to the text; and on the other hand, this same voice is cut up, made discontinuous, ribbed by the intermittent interjections of the one who lends him an ear, that is to say, the one to whom the reading is addressed, the one we have called the *readee*.

In Court

(*Madame Bovary*)

Before we continue sounding out the foursome of forces that sub-
tend the reading scene (those forces that negotiate and determine
the micropolitics of reading), let us make a quick detour, stopping
for a brief look into a courtroom.

We have already caught a glimpse of a certain contiguity
between the ways vocal roles are distributed in reading and the
proclamation of the law: remember how, in classical Greece, the
internalizing the anagnost's reading voice was contemporary with
the internalizing of the archon's voice. And our visit to *Philosophy
in the Bedroom* has just reminded us that the imperative to read can
be if not identical to, at least so close as to be easily mistaken for
the voice Kant described as that of the "prosecutor" (*den Ankläger*)
within us, the public prosecutor or prosecuting attorney whose
vociferations are impossible to drown out, even if they are silent
and remain deep in one's conscience.

We now turn to a real courtroom, to a hearing in the criminal
court of Paris on January 29, 1857. Let us listen first to Monsieur
Ernest Pinard making the case for the prosecution and then to Maître Sénard speaking for the defense. The one who stands accused is
Gustave Flaubert for his novel *Madame Bovary*. A little later, on the
seventh of February, the verdict will ring out: not guilty.[1]

Both the lawyers for the prosecution and those for the defense claim to be concerned with the interests of the presumed readers, mostly with those "young ladies" whose morality might be damaged or, on the contrary, fortified by the novel.[2] And yet, both the "imperial prosecutor" and the "defense" attorney address their speeches to "Gentlemen," to those they have to first and foremost to convince, the magistrates and members of the jury. For now, I must leave aside the matter of women's place in the history of reading and, more generally still, the question of gender or sexual difference in a philosophical anagnosology. (I will come back to it at length when we read *If on a Winter's Night*, where Italo Calvino stages the adventures of a male reader and a female reader.)

Unlike others who have studied the *Madame Bovary* trial, I will not attempt here to shed light either on the novel itself or on its reception. What I am interested in is the juridical stage as a scene of reading or nonreading, as a stage where the very act of reading is negotiated between antagonist forces. To put it succinctly, the courtroom is a projection of the internal phonodrama that plays out within each of us every time we read. Or to look at it from the other perspective (as Svenbro suggests in his anthropology of reading in ancient Greece), we could consider that in becoming silent readers, we internalized a courtroom drama.

From the start, Ernest Pinard, the imperial prosecutor, speaking to the Gentlemen of the jury, admits in his speech that "the public ministry faces a difficulty" that is not due to the "very nature of prevention" — that the book "undermines Religion or Morality" — but instead to the "scope of the work" in question since it is a matter of "the whole of a novel." It is hard to suppress a smile when Pinard asks with the utmost seriousness:

> What is to be done in such a case? What is the duty of the Public Ministry? To read the whole romance? That's impossible. On the other hand, to read only the incriminating texts would expose us to deep reproach. They could say to us: If you do not show the case in all its parts, if you pass over that which precedes and that which follows the incriminating passages it is evident that you wish to suppress the debate by restricting the ground of discussion.[3]

As he addresses these "Gentlemen" to whom the reading he is about to give is addressed — the readees — Pinard wonders whether he should obey the absolute and hyperbolic imperative that dictates that he should read everything, in which case, he would be a sort of anagnost phonograph, incapable of "incriminating," that is to say interrupting, criticizing, commenting on what he reads. (Miming the "Kant with Sade" lexicon, we could say that by fully obeying the categorical imperative to read, the reader that he is would tend to constitute an undivided textual or anagnosological body, not crossed out, with no limits to what it can suffer.) However, Pinard also wonders whether it is legitimate to disobey the imperative, if it is right to cut up, to segment the text as one wishes (to poke holes in it and sew it up, we might say, thinking of the end of *Philosophy in the Bedroom*). Stuck in an impasse, he seems to oscillate like a compass needle attracted by two opposite magnetic fields, as though stretched between two branches of a V: he can neither obey nor disobey the imperative to read, so that reading will be for him a constant negotiation with this double bind that is impossible to satisfy.

Pinard is not the only one to have found himself thus, in a courtroom, facing the imperative to read everything. A century later, during a trial on January 10, 1957, Maître Maurice Garçon had to grapple with the same imperative as he defended Jean-Jacques Pauvert, who was accused of having "sold, distributed, and disseminated" works "contrary to public morality" — the works of the Marquis de Sade. In his speech for the defense, addressed again to "Gentlemen" (there were no more women at reading's trial in 1957 than there had been in 1857), Garçon thus admitted that "Sade's work is often discouraging to read. Personally, I soon gave up on this generally repulsive reading."[4]

In his indictment of *Madame Bovary*'s author, Pinard also gives up on reading in the end. Granted, at first, as he began to speak, he had seemed to believe that he would be able at least partially to obey the reading imperative: "There is but one course to follow," he declared, "and that is to relate to you the whole story of the romance without reading any of it, or pointing out any incriminating passage; then to cite any incriminating texts."[5] (Note that telling is thus not considered reading, but that a comma seems to make incriminating by citing into a synonym for "reading.")

And yet Pinard seems, little by little, to recognize that obeying a categorical imperative in part is, in the end, not to obey it at all. When faced with a categorical imperative, it has to be all or nothing. As he speaks, Pinard progressively gives up on any pretense of having read and starts to slough off the obligation to do so on the Gentlemen who sit in court. "This is the romance," he says at first. "I have related it to you, suppressing no scene in it"[6] (but we already know that, as far as he is concerned, telling is not the same as reading). He continues: "Gentlemen, the first part of my task is fulfilled. I have related, I shall now cite. . . . I will be brief, for you will read the entire romance. I shall limit myself to citing four scenes, or rather four tableaux."[7] While at the beginning of the speech, quoting seemed to be a possible synonym for reading, that is obviously no longer the case here. The task of reading is henceforth devolved to the gentlemen of the jury and the magistrates ("you will read"). It is as if, being impossible to satisfy, the categorical imperative to read is destined to circulate, to be palmed off on others, to slip through scenes.

It is worth noting in passing that according to Pinard, the printers must also submit to this imperative, even as they, too, are destined to betray it: "Printers should read; when they do not read or have read what they print, it is at their own risk and peril. Printers are not machines . . . they are responsible."[8] In this trial, in which the accused is decidedly the novel, rather than the author, three people are charged: "The author of the book," but also Léon Laurent-Pichat, the manager of the *Revue de Paris* in which the novel was serialized, and Auguste-Alexis Pillet, the printer. According to Pinard, the latter is not simply a mechanized anagnost in the age of the printing press, a mere instrument for reading. Rather, he is supposed himself to read, read in the strong sense that Pinard is tempted to attribute to the term, which involves being able to incriminate, judge, in sum, interrupt in a critical sense. However, just as the imperial attorney can, printers can delegate their reading ("when they do not read or have read," says Pinard). Whereas it seemed he should be an anagnost, the printer would then become the readee of another who reads for him.

Not only, then, does the imperative to read slip around and get passed around, it also divides those through whom it passes, making them oscillate between opposite positions assigned alternately: reading or not reading, reading or requiring another to read.

The trial moves forward.

After Pinard sums up for the prosecution, the imperative, with its inflexible demand for total reading, returns to haunt Flaubert's lawyer, Maître Senard. As he puts it, "To ask the judges to read an entire romance would be asking too much; but we are before judges who love truth, who desire the truth, and who to learn it would not shrink from any fatigue. We are before judges who desire justice and desire it energetically, and who will read, without any kind of hesitation, what we beg them to read."[9] Indeed, Maître Senard's long speech for the defense will tend to fill in the blanks left by the preceding incrimination during the prosecutor's speech. And as though reading could never be full enough, as though the anagnosological imperative operated without respite, Flaubert's lawyer seems seriously to consider the possibility that two readings, rather than one, might be required: "I ask you, gentlemen, if your first reading has left you in doubt, to give it a second reading."[10]

However, even within this speech guided by the idea of an indivisible, continuous, and incessantly repeated reading, the cut reasserts its law. As we will see, the interruption weaves its way in and out in a manner not dissimilar to the ellipsis that punctures or pricks the end of *Philosophy in the Bedroom*.

Compare the two occurrences of the verb "to read" conjugated in the imperative in Maître Senard's speech.

"Read,"[11] the lawyer first says, and indeed then reads aloud, for the benefit of the magistrates and members of the jury who are his readees, a first passage from *Madame Bovary* devoted to Emma's childhood and the books that make her dream. "Is this lascivious, gentlemen?" he asks, as he interrupts his reading for a moment. He then begins again with another imperative, equivalent to the first: "Let us continue."[12]

The second time, however, the same imperative, "Let us read,"[13] announces and initiates the reading of a passage that describes Emma on her deathbed. And this time, when the lawyer interrupts his reading, it is to confess that he is overwhelmed, flooded with feeling: "I could not read it . . . it is impossible for me to continue this reading."[14] The one who wanted to fill in the gaps left by the previous speech ends up adding more gaps. And why is it that he thus begins to puncture the texts he had meant to suture?

The hole, the gap into which the lawyer-reader disappears for a moment, is the discontinuity onto which, paradoxically, his total reading is inscribed. For it is precisely when he is saturated by the text, when he is submerged by what he is reading, that the reader faints, swooning like Sade's victims, at the very moment when he reaches his fulfillment. Reading as pure passion (*pur pâtir*), its intensity undamaged by the interruptions of, or for, the other, lapses into the nonreading wherein the reader disappears.

Reading Genders

(*If on a Winter's Night a Traveler*)

Perhaps, dear reader [*chère lectrice, cher lecteur*], you remember: at the very beginning of this book that you are holding in your hands, I asked you whether or not you had already begun to read or whether you were preparing to do so. No doubt you thought it was a funny question: in order to answer it, I must have already read that question, thus the answer is presupposed by its very enunciation.

Now, here, I am in roughly the same situation as you were then. Preparing to read certain passages with you, I open Italo Calvino's novel, *If on a Winter's Night a Traveler*. And here is what I read (it is the first sentence): "You are about to begin reading Italo Calvino's new novel, *If on a Winter's Night a Traveler*. Relax. Concentrate."[1]

This beginning is dizzying. It seems so simple, and yet it deserves a place in the history of literature alongside Proust's "For a long time, I went to bed early'" and a few other first sentences. What does it say? What does it do? It addresses me, me its reader, speaking to me in the second person singular. And this undifferentiated "you" — he or she, we do not know — is already reading what he or she has not yet begun to read. That is the disjointed but elastic temporality of such an opening: "You are about to start reading" — reading what? Reading the very novel that you have been reading since the beginning of this sentence that tells you that you are about to begin. We are already reading what we will only begin to read now, that is now, I mean now, now that we have already read it.

The time of this now, which is sustained by and through the tension between an already and a not yet, is that of the gap within the reader, between the male reader and himself, between the female reader and herself, or, perhaps, between the male reader and female reader or between the female reader and the male reader that I am, between she and he or he and she who both inhabit the "you" to whom the incipit is addressed. As Calvino writes in a letter to a critic that was published in 1979 (the same year as the novel), the "hero" of *If on a Winter's Night*... is that "average reader" (*lettore medio*) one can consider the "natural addressee of the novel." He immediately adds: "Double hero, since the hero is split into a male Reader and a female Reader" (*protagonista doppio, perché si scinde in un Lettore et in una Lettrice*).[3]

What awaits us in this novel on whose threshold we are suspended is thus a question, a question that is coming back at us from where we had temporarily abandoned it, in the middle of the assembly of "Gentlemen" at *Madame Bovary's* trial or the Sade court case: What about gender in reading?

We cannot, we can no longer, ask this question in a simple and naïve or even crude way, as though what were at stake were readers whose identity, including sexual identity, was given once and for all. We know that all the voices inhabiting the reading scene (*erastēs, erōmenos*, anagnost, imperative, readee) take cues from each other and mix together ceaselessly each time in a specific way that *constitutes* the reader, produces the reader. To borrow a phrase from Derrida, we might say that "the reader does not exist," not so much because the reader has to be "constructed, even engendered, let's say *invented* by the work," but because the reader does not exist before *the reading*.[4]

Calvino's opening gives exemplary and dizzying resonance to the fact that every time I read, the reading invents me precisely in the gap — of anticipation or delay — whereby I come before myself and I follow myself. "You are about to start reading," that is to say, to become the he or she produced by the very "reading" of which the "you" at the beginning of the sentence was not yet (yet already partially) the subject.

When we ask after gender in reading, we must immediately add another question: How does sexual difference or gender relate to the deferral through which reading anticipates or delays itself? Or, better, how does it produce the self as anticipation or delay? If it is the case that there are no constituted readers before the reading that invents them, it cannot be, strictly speaking, that the reader's gender is a given.

Gender, as one of the things at stake in reading, actually comes from much further back than 1957 (the Sade court case) or 1857 (*Madame Bovary* trial). We did not cross paths with any women among the *erastai*, *eromênoi*, or anagnosts reading in ancient Greece. Granted, here and there, we can catch glimpses of women caught reading, female readers whose anagnosological portraits have left a mark in the historical archive. Think, for example, of the portrait Lucian of Samosata left us of Panthéa, emperor Lucius Verus's mistress, as she reads: "In her hands was an open scroll; half read (so I surmised) and half to be read."[5] Nevertheless, although we can of course cite a few exceptional figures, the figures of female readers handed down to posterity (think of Christine de Pizan, who, in her *Livre de la Cité des dames*, written in 1405, "is much surprised by the opinion put forth by some men who assert that they would not want their daughters, wives, or kinswomen to be educated"),[6] there is no escaping the fact: as such, women have been massively and relentlessly kept away from any right to read.

The French revolutionary and writer Pierre Sylvain Maréchal's claim to fame is only to have provided a formulation of this exclusion that is more explicit than most. In 1801, he submitted to the "head of households, fathers, and husbands" his *Project for a Law Forbidding Teaching Women to Read*. An endless list of hundred and thirteen reasons precede the actual formulation of the law, which stipulates that "women (girls, married or widowed) never poke their nose into a book." Here is one: "Considering that nature herself, by endowing women with a prodigious aptitude for talking, seems to have wanted to spare them the trouble of learning to read."[7] Oral expression for women, access to writing for men.[8]

Given that this anagnosological prohibition weighed on women for so many centuries, it is not surprising that the competition, rivalry, or emulation between a female and a male reader is rarely staged. And if it is, the chances are that it simply confirms the aforementioned appraisal. Thus, when the writer Jean Paul publishes his review of Madame de Staël's *Of Germany*, he is intent on defending a certain number of German literary monuments whom he considers to have been unfairly treated by the "intellectual amazon."[9] After advocating for Goethe's *Faust*, which de Staël had criticized for its chaotic inspiration, and apparently intending to defend a national masterpiece, he asks a question whose violence projects well beyond the literary debate that is its context: "Readeresses, why will every one of you insist on thinking herself a reader?"[10]

I have recalled, all too briefly, this long tradition of androcentric anagnosology because Calvino's "average reader," that average reader who is bound to be divided into a male reader and a female reader, certainly inherits many of its traits. One might even fear that this average reader inherits the worst clichés of the tradition. Indeed, when the reading woman does appear, it is against a backdrop of a plethora of books, as though to signify that she reads a lot, that is to say too much, much too much: "You appeared for the first time to the Reader [*Lettore*] in a bookshop; you took shape, detaching yourself from a wall of shelves, as if the quantity of books made the presence of a young lady Reader [*Lettrice*] necessary."[11]

The female reader thus essentially appears as an overreader (like Emma Bovary), she who reads in the domestic sphere to which she is assigned and within which the kitchen is a special enclave: "Your house, being the place in which you read, can tell us the position books occupy in your life.... To understand this, our Reader knows that the first step is to visit the kitchen. The kitchen is the part of the house that can tell the most things about you."[12]

As we might also have expected, the female reader in *If on a Winter's Night* . . . confirms the platitude according to which a woman reads for the ephemeral pleasure of confused entertainment: "The function of books for you is immediate reading; they are not instruments of study or reference or components of a library arranged according to some order."[13] She is clearly not a "Reader Who Rereads,"[14] rather, one who consumes the works that pass through her hands. She even reads more than one at a time, which makes her an unfaithful, fickle reader: "Numerous volumes are scattered, some left open, others with makeshift bookmarks or corners of the pages folded down. Obviously, you have the habit of reading several books at the same time."[15]

The final touch, which clearly tethers the lady reader to an androcentric anagnosology, betrays her inconstant nature, not to say a Bovarian threat of adultery: "Reader, prick up your ears," says the narrator, taking distinct pleasure in infusing "this suspicion," an "anxiety as a jealous man" in the one he addresses, on the grounds that she who is "reader of several books at once" also — the connection seems inextricable — "tends to carry forward, at the same time, other stories also."[16]

The stereotypical aspects of this portrait of the female reader are undeniable and warrant underlining. However, it is just as undeniable that, in *If on a Winter's Night,* . . . gender cannot be considered to be a given, the result of some prior and irrevocable distribution. This is made clear, for instance, by a few lines that, if read closely, should prohibit any stable assignation to a fixed sexual identity. These lines come in parentheses as a sort of aside by the narrator, who is talking to the (male) reader as though to console him for no longer being the exclusive center of attention: "(Don't believe that the book is losing sight of you, Reader [*Lettore*]. The you that was shifted to the Other Reader [*Lettrice*] can, at any sentence, be addressed to you again. You are always a possible you)."[17]

You are always a possible you. This is as dizzying as the incipit ("You are about to begin to read...") that it echoes in so many ways. With this address, the narrator does not simply signify to the (male) reader that he is one of the two possibilities given a predefined binary choice (masculine or feminine). He does not simply tell him that having been temporarily downgraded in favor of that other "you," the female reader, the male reader should not worry anymore, that he will again become the main, if not the only, addressee.

If we take a closer look, the delay or anticipation of itself with which the book opened ("You are about to...") plays out again over gender. Indeed, the first "you" of the sentence ("You are always...") has merely the empty general sense of an address. Only the second "you" ("a possible you") has undergone the process of specification that determines a particular "you," distinguished by being opposed to the other one. If it is the case, as we maintained earlier, that readers do not preexist the reading (each time I read, the reading invents me), then neither does their gender: each time I read (each time I am interpellated as "you"), I am in the process of becoming a female reader or a male reader.

And such is the case each time I reread this sentence — "You are always a possible you" — which is exemplary of how all the others operate. Each "you" (even if it is only implicit), can, with each sentence, be "a possible you," the same or the other one, each time.

———❧———

We are, then, here facing a feedback loop that looks much like the one at the beginning of the book ("You are about to start reading..."). As an "average reader" divided between a male reader and a female reader, "you" is divided again, each of the gendered alternatives are divided again each time that he or she rereads (rereading, as we saw in Plato's *Phaedrus*, being what permutes or switches the roles, notably those of the *erastēs* and the *erōmenos*). Each time, the female reader and the male reader are divided again, recut (we might say resexed), again and again, by the difference that already constituted them.

Does this mean that sexual difference is somehow neutralized by some logic that we know will end up serving one of the two genders, generally the masculine one? Granted, Calvino does not always escape this danger, as for instance when, in the letter to a critic, he writes that the male reader does not have "precise identity and tastes," that he is as it were unmarked, whereas the female reader "knows how to explain her expectations and what she refuses" (in terms, let it be noted, "as far as possible from any form of intellectualism," since she reads "out of passion").[18] Neutral, nongendered reading would in the end be, as we might expect, masculine reading, the universal form (whereas feminine reading would be subject to individual passions).

If, however, there is a tendency — or rather, a tension — in the novel toward the neutral, it cannot be reduced to the kind of anagnosology that can barely hide its androcentrism under the veil of universalism. Listen to the intensity with which Calvino's characters sometimes pursue the idea — the quest or the question — of a reading that could overcome its gendered difference: "Will we be able to say 'today it is reading' as we say 'today it is raining'?"[19] asks Silas Flannery, the Irish writer whose diary constitutes chapter eight of *If on a Winter's Night* . . . .

What matters here is not only the future tense of the question ("Will we be able to say?"), but also the fact that subject disappears. Indeed, whereas in English, an impersonal "it" is necessary, in Italian, one can simply elide the pronoun altogether: *piove* is the way to say "it is raining." I insist on both the future and the elision or eclipse of the reading subject in order to underline that the neuter of "it reads" is neither an originary indetermination that will at some later stage be divided into two genders (masculine and feminine) nor a stable and pacified state that could be reached by overcoming the opposition of the two sexes.

It is impossible to attribute this reading to anyone; it is what is yet to come *ahead of the text and ahead of the reading subject.* It is what barely appears on the horizon, now, and now, and now . . . between you and you, between you who are already reading and you who are about to start reading what you are reading, between the reading "you" that you are and the other "you" that reading can lead you to be. *In this between, there is reading.* The infinitive of the event of reading as becoming.[20] It arises, it ascends from the intensification, the proliferation of differences, from one you to the other until they tend toward a pure deferral/differing, until the difference tends to go, so to speak, faster — or beyond — its terms.

Indeed, what happens when, in chapter two, the male reader, having noticed that his copy of *If on a Winter's Night . . .* is defective, decides to take it back to the bookstore to exchange it for another? What happens at the exact moment when the book that I am thus *reading myself reading* (yes, that is what is happening: I read that the male reader that I am reads *If on a Winter's Night . . .*) is about to be replaced by another that, under the same title, will differ from itself?

It is at precisely this moment that the female reader appears among the aisles and shelves of the bookstore, a double of the reading "you" that I am: "And so the Other Reader [*Lettrice*] makes her happy entrance into your field of vision, Reader [*Lettore*], or, rather, into the field of your attention; or, rather, you have entered a magnetic field from whose attraction you cannot escape."[21] The henceforth magnetized space of reading has become triangulated, and the division of the "average reader" (split into a male reader and a female reader, facing the text and face to face) kindles the reading infinitive that flows through and disjoins the reading "you."

The reading "you" is not a stable identity, an accomplished individuation; it has no name, no determining characteristics: "Who you are, Reader, your age, your status, profession, income: that would be indiscreet to ask."[22] Neither, however, is the reading "you" a mere generality that can hardly hide its specificity; it is rather the singularity of a disposition to read that, although it cannot be determined in an individualized form, is not an empty universalizable container: "What counts is the state of your spirit now, in the privacy of your home, as you try to re-establish perfect calm in order to sink back again into the book."[23] Here and now, affected in a singular way, the "you" prepares to read within a force field that is all the more strongly magnetized as the differences — and not the identities — are sharpened or, better, accelerate.

Indeed — and we are coming to this — the novel describes the polarization created by the appearance of the female reader within the reading scene in terms of speed. Since she arrived, since her appearance upset everything, reading is a newly intense experience:

> Something has changed since yesterday. Your reading is no longer solitary: you think of the Other Reader [*Lettrice*], who, at this same moment is also opening the book; and there, the novel to be read is superimposed by a possible novel to be lived.... This is how you have changed since yesterday, you who insisted you preferred a book ... to a real-life experience, always elusive, discontinuous, debated. Does this mean that the book has become an instrument, a channel of communication, a rendez-vous? This does not mean its reading will grip you less: on the contrary, something has been added to its powers.[24]

By attracting the reader from the novel to be read toward the novel to be lived, this triangulation, which seems to distract the reader from his reading, actually reinforces and invigorates the infinitive power of reading. And it does so, as I was saying, by imparting an acceleration, as we learn from the extraordinary fourth chapter, which begins precisely with remarks on the speed of reading vocalization: "Listening to someone read aloud is very different from reading in silence. When you read, you can stop or skip sentences: you are the one who sets the pace. When someone else is reading, it is difficult to make your attention coincide with the tempo of his reading: the voice goes either too fast or too slow."[25]

Yet as we have insisted repeatedly along the journey from "The Sandman" to the Sade trial, reading in silence involves differences in vocal speeds just as much as reading aloud does, insofar as the voices that inhabit the reading scene, far from being erased, are internalized. In the innermost recesses of my male or female reader self, a reading voice may therefore also be too fast or too slow because it is drawn, attracted, magnetized, by others within the diverging phonic force field they compose.

We also see this in the rest of chapter four, when a certain professor reads, or rather translates out loud, that is to say, improvises orally, while the male and female readers listen, the translation of a text written in a language that has disappeared. Both readers hence share the readee's role, whereas the professor is more or less discharging the functions of the anagnost (granted, this anagnost also produces glosses or interpretations). What we have here is thus a differentiation, an additional ramification of the reading scene where the readee divides into two "you"s, one male, who remains nameless, and the other female, named Ludmilla.

The narrator attributes this scission of the readee to a speed differential; it is the result of excess haste:

> Ludmilla is always at least one step ahead of you. "I like to know that books exist that I will still be able to read . . . ," she says, sure that existent objects, concrete albeit unknown, must correspond to the strength of her desire. How can you keep up with her, this woman who is always reading another book besides the one before her eyes, a book that does not yet exist, but which, since she wants it, cannot fail to exist?[26]

Clearly, the differential that splits the readee is both a gender differential and a velocity differential, where these two differentials are inextricably linked to one another. And in the high-speed chase between these two "you"s, he or she running ahead of the other, the infinitive of reading accelerates until it is about to take off from the text, to take leave of the text to project ahead of it, toward the "book that does not yet exist," as though reading could overtake its object to become pure reading (just reading rather than reading this or that).

Soon, we will learn from de Certeau to call this an absolute reading (*absolutum* in Latin means precisely "detached, untethered").

―∽

The speed and gender differential that pushes the infinitive of reading beyond the text can also turn into a delay that holds reading back, as at the beginning of chapter seven:

> Your mind is occupied by two simultaneous concerns: the interior one, with your reading, and the other, with Ludmilla, who is late for your appointment. You concentrate on your reading, trying to shift your concern for her to the book, as if hoping to see her come toward you from the pages. But you're no longer able to read, the novel has stalled on the page before your eyes, as if only Ludmilla's arrival could set the chain of events in motion again.[27]

Either delayed or ahead of itself: it seems there is no proper speed for reading, since reading consists precisely of these gaps where you are about to begin reading what you are already reading, you who are always one of the readees—the other one—still to come. Yet insisting, as we have, on the spacing, on the diastole in the reading scene that affects the relationships voices have to one another and to themselves, we might forget that reading is just as much a matter of tightening, of systole, of gathering.

Let us, then, pick up *If on a Winter's Night . . .* again from the start, from the incipit, where everything began to come apart, where a gap appeared between the already and the not yet. Let us reread: "You are about to begin reading Italo Calvino's new novel, *If on a Winter's Night a Traveler*. Relax. Concentrate." The double imperative that comes after the first sentence — "relax" (*rilassati*) and "concentrate" (*raccogliti*) — literally spells out that the diastolic phase of reading (in which the voices move away from one another) must be followed by a systolic phase (in which they draw together, tending to blend into a single voice). Indeed, *raccogliti*, "concentrate," might be a loose translation of the Latin *lege*, the imperative form of the verb *legere*, which means "to pick up, to pick, to roll together, to gather," but also, of course, "to read."

If on a Winter's Night . . . repeatedly oscillates between these anagnosological diastoles and systoles.[28] Indeed, the *end* of the reading, both its ending and its aim, seems to be to fill in the gap that cleaves the readee into two dichotomous figures. In the final brief chapter twelve that closes the novel, the male reader and the female reader are thus brought together, as though they were reading at the same time, as though they had become one:

> Now you are man and wife, Reader and Reader [*Lettore e Lettrice*]. A great double bed [*un grande letto matrimoniale*] receives your parallel readings. Ludmilla closes her book, turns off her light, puts her head back against the pillow and says, "Turn off your light, too. Aren't you tired of reading?" And you say, "Just a moment, I've almost finished *If on a Winter's Night a Traveler* by Italo Calvino."[29]

In Calvino's Italian, the final "bed" that welcomes the two readees becoming one immediately evokes reading: *letto* means "bed," but it is also the past participle of the verb *leggere*, "to read." It is as though, once the reading was completed — or for the reading to be complete — the infinitive of reading becomes a "has been read" at the same time as the two singular "you"s unite in a plural "you." However, we immediately see that this final simultaneity, which the entire novel strove to have us expect and desire, is actually just as deeply riven by the gap that cleaves the readee as was the initial you of the incipit. "You are about to start reading Italo Calvino's new novel," we read, moving away from ourselves as we did, letting the "you" spread out between an already and a not yet.

"I've almost finished *If on a Winter's Night a Traveler*," we now read, not knowing whether the final period really is precisely the end of the reading or whether instead it marks that the end is imminent. The stopping point is thus itself diluted or, more precisely, the stopping point is stretched like an elastic band that at a certain point unknown to us will contract to put the finishing touch on the having read and having been a reader.

Gunther Ranbow, poster for S. Fischer Verlag, 1976
(courtesy of Gunther Ranbow)

Reading, Binding, Unbinding

It is time to gather together what we have picked up or gleaned so far. It is time for the gesture that Gunter Rambow, a German graphic designer, was able so powerfully to illustrate with the poster he designed in 1976 for Fischer, a publisher: the image shows a hand emerging from a book (as a sort of outgrowth) to hold the book shut, binding it.

Picking up, collecting, gathering: these are all possible senses of the Latin verb *legere*. It is as though reading essentially boils down to pulling together, the reader being a sort of binder. Maybe that is what Kierkegaard had in mind when he wrote the preface to *Stages on Life's Way*. Calling out to the "benevolent reader" (*lectori benevolo*), a bookbinder (*bogbinder*) tells of finding a "small package of handwritten papers" (possibly "by several authors"), how he had "stitched them together in a colored paper folder" and then, before publishing them, had read them himself ("in the long winter evenings when I had nothing else to do") and had them "read aloud" by his children so that they could practice deciphering script.[1]

This bookbinder, named Hilarius, is a sort of anticipation of the readers to come that we are. He binds and reads (*lie et lit*) before we do what each of us is about to begin to read and bind in turn. This contrasts with what we find at the other end of the bound volume, where the one who addresses the reader directly again in the few concluding pages ("A Concluding Word") has no name. After all the different fictitious voices that have spoken in turn throughout the work (the pseudonyms in which Kierkegaard revels: Hilarius the bookbinder, William Afham a spouse, Frater Taciturnus), only an anonymous "I" is left to speak out:

> My dear reader — but to whom am I speaking? Perhaps no one at all is left. . . . In the beginning, no doubt, the favorably disposed reader reined in his swift steed and thought I was riding a pacer, but when I did not move from the spot, the horse (that is, the reader) or, if you please, the rider, became impatient, and I was left behind alone: a nonequestrian or a Sunday rider whom everybody outrides.[2]

The one who is speaking to himself here has been left behind by the reader, who at the beginning was preceded by the bookbinder. And whereas one — the bookbinder — was thus a figure of anticipation as a systolic gathering, the other — the narrator who speaks last, and alone — embodies delay as a diastolic spacing.

Any theory of reading must take both of these two contrary movements into account. However, the anagnosology that has come down to us from the tradition massively emphasized gathering over dislocation. This has led to what we can only call a *politics of reading*, as we will verify when we analyze a particular reading machine, namely, Thomas Hobbes's *Leviathan*.

In 1954, in a brief but dense text, "What Is Called Reading?," Martin Heidegger distilled into a short paragraph the essence of all the discourses on reading that consider the act of reading to be an injunction to bind. Reading, he says, is *Sammlung*, a word whose semantic value oscillates between "concentration," "bringing together," "collecting," "selecting," "gathering": "What is [calls forth] reading? That which is sustaining and directive in reading is gatheredness [*Sammlung*]. To what [*worauf*] is it gathered? To what is written, to what is said in writing. Authentic reading [*das eigentliche Lesen*] is a gatheredness to that which, unbeknown to us, has already claimed our essence [*Wesen*], regardless of whether we comply with it or withhold from it."[3]

Forcing a little, as Heidegger himself does, for instance when he translates the Presocratics, one could almost translate *Sammlung* here as "binding" (thinking of Kierkegaard's Hilarius). This suggestion especially makes sense, given that when they were initially published in 1954 in a journal of pedagogy, *Welt der Schule* (The world of school), these first lines were printed on the cover in a reproduction of Heidegger's handwriting. There, it looks as though, in connecting the letters of his script, Heidegger was already binding the volume that his sentences present and carry, wrapping that volume in a way that reminds us of the hand Rambow imagined.

What does Heidegger say to those who are about to open the journal to read and bind the contributions that it has gathered? Reading, he says, is the movement of gathering — a movement of convergence or of concentration — toward or aimed at what speaks through the text. In this account, what comes out of what is written, what offers itself up for hearing, certainly looks like an imperative insofar as we are called on to comply. It is even an imperative that has already requisitioned us (it has "already claimed our essence") without our being aware ("unbeknown to us"). Something has already called on us to read, says Heidegger, even if we have not yet heard the call, even if we are not yet responding, even if our reading is not yet "authentic" (*eigentlich*).

Although the words may be unusual, they seem to express commonplace thoughts about reading as an exercise in gathering, an attention to capturing what is said in the text. Yet we should maybe not go too fast here and instead listen carefully to the peculiar construction of the paragraph.

Indeed, what is striking is the impersonal character of the first four sentences. They talk about reading — *das Lesen* is a substantivized infinitive form — rather than the reader, as though what matters is first and foremost the "it is reading" that a character in *If on a Winter's Night . . .* construed by analogy with "it is raining." It is only in the fifth sentence, whose main subject is again the nominalized verb, that "we" makes a late and almost reticent appearance in the form of a possessive adjective ("our") and a pronoun ("we").

The "we" who finally makes it to this strangely depopulated reading scene seems thus to be a latecomer, as though reading, drawn by the gatheredness that carries it ahead of itself, had preceded, overtaken that "we" straggling behind like an empty shell. Or maybe we should say that something of that "we" (its "essence" [*Wesen*]) has already been gripped, carried away by the movement of the reading, so that the reading "we" is delayed with respect to itself. Be that as it may, "we" is, as "you" was at the beginning of Calvino's incipit, suspended in an interval in which "we" is already reading what "we" does not yet really read. In this sense, the gathering (*Sammlung*) Heidegger refers to and describes as what guides reading would also be aimed at making the reading "we" coincide with itself.

In *What Is Thinking?* — a course given in 1951–1952 and published in 1954 (the same year as "What Is Reading?"), Heidegger recalls that like the Greek verb *legein* or the Latin *legere*, the German verb for "reading," *lesen*, also signifies to collect or to gather: "Reading . . . is done by gathering [*versammeln*] the letters. Without this gathering [*Versammeln*], without a gleaning [*die Lese*] in the sense in which wheat or grapes are gleaned [*Ähren- und Weinlese*], we should never be able to read [*lesen*] a single word, however keenly we observe the written signs."[4] One should not, however, rush to the conclusion that this reading gathering, or this gathering reading, necessarily involves a slow and continuously increasing concentration that leads toward what is said in writing.

Although I cannot do justice here to the Heideggerian way of reading, exemplified notably in his long meditations on Friedrich Hölderlin's poems, we can at least hold onto a claim he explicitly made in one of his readings, the one devoted to Georg Trakl's poetry in a conference whose title was "Language in the Poem" (given in 1952 and published in 1953, that is, a year before "What Is Reading?"). Here, at the very moment when he insists on the "site" (*Ort*) around which the poetic language "gathers" (*versammelt*), Heidegger declares that he will lead our attention toward it "as if by a sudden leap of insight," that is, via a sort of ocular saccade (via what should be translated literally as a "gazeleap," [*Blicksprung*]).[5]

There is thus speed — and even the infinite speed of an elliptical leap — in the gathering toward the site where the poem's statement gathers as if at its tip. (An old sense of the term *Ort*, Heidegger reminds us, was the pointed end of a tool or a weapon — a spear, for example.) Even in its hyperbolic version in the form of a Heideggerian collectedness or gathering, the systole seems always to include a diastole. In these circumstances, no one can say whether it is a patient constriction toward focus or, rather, a sudden jolt, a leap, a gap.

While Heidegger propounded his theory of a gathering reading (albeit one striated by jolts), Maurice Blanchot published a short article in *La Nouvelle revue française* in May 1953 under the sober title *Lire*, which has been translated as "Reading," but is in fact the infinitive of the verb — not "reading," but "to read."[6]

The title stands out against the white page and floats, suspended, above the first line of the text. "A word — an infinitive marked by the infinite — without subject," as Blanchot said elsewhere.[7] This meditation on reading is thus from the start in the register of an impersonal reading that is not far from the "it is reading" that Calvino taught us to hear as we would an "it is raining."

Indeed, Blanchot's infinitive gestures toward a sort of pure reading that appeals to the reader only the better to erase him, the better to absorb him into a becoming work that strips the text (the book) of any author, perhaps of any history:

> The reader is himself always fundamentally anonymous. He is any reader, none in particular, unique but transparent. He does not add his name to the book (as our fathers did long ago); rather, he erases every name from it by his nameless presence, his modest, passive gaze, interchangeable and insignificant, under whose light pressure the book appears written, separate from everything and everyone. Reading makes of the book what the sea and the wind make of objects fashioned by men: a smoother stone, a fragment fallen from the sky without a past, without a future.... The book needs the reader in order to become a statue. It needs the reader if it is to declare itself a thing without an author and hence without a reader.[8]

Blanchot's reader thus ends up being dissolved into a reading that he does not sign, a reading of which he is not the sovereign subject. One could, of course, say that this reading infinitive has an imperative value for the reader (it is easy to imagine that an invisible exclamation mark punctuates the title: *Lire!*, "Read!"). If, however, it is an imperative, it is a particular kind of imperative since it does not command an action, an act, or an activity: it only prescribes that what is coming be welcomed with a "yes," that a "yes" greet the work as it affirms itself.

This is thus a peculiar imperative, one that deserves its own place in the fascinating history of all the reading imperatives we have glimpsed, from the one Eucleides addresses to the anagnost in the *Theaetetus* to the mother's prescription in the epigraph to *Philosophy in the Bedroom*. Indeed, the object of this imperative oscillates in a way that remains undecidable between active and passive, a letting happen rather than a proper "making happen" (*faire*). This is why Blanchot adds quotation marks to this verb, to signal that it has lost its power:

The singular property of reading demonstrates the singular sense of the verb "to make" [*faire*] in the expression "it makes the work become a work." The word *make* here does not designate a productive activity. Reading does not produce anything, does not add anything. It lets be what is. It is freedom: not the freedom that produces being or grasps it, but freedom that welcomes, consents, says yes, can say only yes, and, in the space opened by this yes, lets the work's overwhelming decisiveness affirm itself, lets be its affirmation that it is — and nothing more.[9]

What Blanchot, a little further on, calls "the light, innocent Yes of reading,"[10] is thus, in the end, a yes that precedes itself, gets ahead of itself: it is a yes that "lets...affirm itself...its affirmation," and that therefore says *yes to the yes* that it is.

This assent to assent, or this affirmation of the affirmation — two terms that are of course not synonymous and that, as I will show, are separated by the difference between passive and active[11] — this redoubling of an assent that anticipates itself, is exactly what also happens between the title and the incipit of Blanchot's text as they perform, under our eyes, reading's specific anticipation of itself. At the beginning, there is the repetition of the French infinitive whose first occurrence (the title) is outside the text (as was the reading prescription in Sade), whereas the second is the beginning of the text:

Reading [*Lire*]
      Reading [*Lire*]: in the writer's logbook we are not surprised to come upon...[12]

The text begins by repeating the quasi-imperative of the title (*lire!*, "read!"), which is then immediately punctuated by a colon that opens the infinitive (*lire*) toward all that will follow, all the words and pages to come ("reading: in the writer's logbook..."), assenting in advance to their arrival. *Lire — lire* ("read[ing] — read[ing]"): it is as though reading had already said "yes," "yes" to this reading that it is, even before reading *something*, this or that, these words or those phrases.

And that is why, in this being ahead of itself, in this "yes" to the "yes" that it is, reading is, from the start, carried away by a movement that projects it beyond the text. *Already beyond*, as these remarkable lines from Blanchot suggest: "There is in reading, at least *at reading's point of departure* [emphasis mine: in other words, in the redoubling that means that it has already begun, in this departure that is in no sense punctual since it is not one and indivisible like a point], something vertiginous that resembles...a leap [how can one avoid thinking of Heidegger's *Blicksprung*, the saccade in that text on Trakl that was also published in 1953?], an infinite leap: I want *to read* what is, however, not written [the verb *to read* is here in italics, insisting by distinguishing itself typographically from the text, as though it persists in its movement even as its object, what is written, is disappearing]."[13]

Reading what is however not written: Blanchot has just quoted, without naming it, and perhaps without meaning to, a phrase of Hugo von Hofmannsthal's to which we will return. (As we will see, Benjamin reprises it several times in contexts that will turn out to be decisive for our study.) Blanchot diverts the phrase from its context in order to gesture toward what gives reading its impulse to move *beyond what is written*, however paradoxical that might sound.[14] Reading does not do so by breaking radically away from what is written (it is not a matter of the reader being purely distracted or interrupted), but by making its way *through what is written and ahead of it*: referring to the "real book" that is subjected to a "real reading," Blanchot thus writes that "when it is read, it has never been read before. *It does not come into its presence as a work except in the space opened by this unique reading,* each time the first and each time the only."[15] It is as though, common sense notwithstanding, the writing that one reads is constituted as a work in the wake or after the fact of its reading: the reading must, then, precede the work.

No doubt one should then say that reading is both that anticipation of itself that projects it ahead of the text and at the same time a delay with respect to itself, which means that its progression through the work is, at the outset, a rereading.[16]

Reading that involves clearing a path that carries the reader beyond the written text: this is an idea with which de Certeau also grappled when he tried to think what he called an *absolute reading*. However, the idea appears in his work after he has undertaken a protracted liberation of the reader, in stark contrast with the strange and paradoxical freedom of which Blanchot spoke, that "freedom . . . which cannot but say 'yes.'" (One would be justified in thinking that it strongly resembles a form of obedience, the very old model for which is the anagnost.)

Against "scriptural imperialism,"[17] against the domination of the text understood as a productive activity (like the activity of the *erastēs* in classical Greece) that reduces "the assimilation in reading to a passivity" (that of the *erōmenos*), de Certeau consistently affirms and underlines the "autonomy of the practice of reading" and "the reader's creativity."[18] Granted, what he calls the "inventiveness" of "reading operations" contribute to the becoming work that Blanchot attributed to reading as the pure clearing of a path: for de Certeau, also, it is the reader who, without in any way taking "the position of the author," without rewriting the texts, "detaches them from their origin (lost or accidental),"[19] unburdens them, unbinds them. In the end, however, it is not exactly, as it was in Blanchot, the text that thus becomes absolute (that is, unhitched, unchained), thanks to reading, by breaking away from the nets cast by the author and the circumstances of its genesis. Rather, for de Certeau, reading liberates *itself* from the written text as the "ground that determined it." And this newly conquered freedom should be understood here in the simplest and most classical sense of the term (the most unquestioned, also), as a form of "autonomy." The reading voice is no longer condemned to be the "body of the other" (as in the case of the anagnost lending his vocal organ). Instead, it is "unmoor[ed] from the scriptural place";[20] it is freed from the mooring thanks in part to the speed that reading can develop:

> The autonomy of the eye suspends the body's complicities with the text; it . . . increases the reader's possibilities of moving about. One index of this: the methods of speed reading. Just as the airplane makes possible a growing independence with respect to the constraints imposed by geographical organization, the techniques of speed reading obtain, through the rarefaction of the eye's stopping points, an acceleration of its movements across the page, an autonomy in relation to the determinations of the text and a multiplication of the spaces covered.[21]

Among the authors who have made serious attempts at producing an anagnosology worthy of the name, de Certeau is, as far as I know, the only one not to have peremptorily swept aside the issue of speed reading, a matter with which we will be more and more concerned here. Not only will we, with de Certeau, consider speed as an effect of modernity ("to read without uttering the words aloud or at least mumbling them is a 'modern' experience, unknown for millennia,"[22] he writes); not only will we pay attention to speed because, in this acceleration of reading that Valéry will repeatedly denounce, what is at stake is *what is left of the voice*; above all, we will attend to the matter of speed because it requires us to think what must be called the *tangency* of reading, the point where reading takes off from the written text while still touching it.

In a text the first version of which was written at roughly the same time as "Reading as Poaching," de Certeau tries to understand and describe under the term "'absolute' reading," this point where reading becomes tangential to the page, thus named "because it frees itself from the text and, in so doing, absolves itself from its law."[23] The emblematic gesture of this tangential reading is that of Teresa of Ávila when she declares: "I would open the book with no need for anything more" or that of her spiritual mentor, John of Ávila, who advises: "With your eyes fixed on the book, do not attach your heart to it."[24] Having quoted these instructions gleaned from mystical treatises that enjoin the reader to detach from the book, de Certeau offers the following commentary: "A diffuse attention maintains a horizon of the absolute. It cannot be held within the textual enclosure; it considers the pages of the book as places of transit that must be abandoned one after another."[25]

In this mystical practice of reading as tangency, de Certeau discerns, buried in a past that demands to be reactivated, the possibility of "emancipat[ing] the reader-subject," of crediting him "with an existence of his own, detached from any subjugation or conformity to the book."[26] Of course, at first glance, one might fear that aiming for a pure and simple liberation of the reader, claiming the autonomy of a sovereign subject for the reader, might constitute a move backward. Is this a regression compared with the always repeated individuation of the reader from the impersonal infinitive of reading such as we encountered it in Calvino, for instance ("you are always a possible you")? We might fear that reducing the "it is reading" to the reassuring illusion of an "I read" whose rights are to be reasserted would preclude considering the infinite becoming of a reader who individualizes himself in the course of his reading.

A closer look, however, makes it clear that these fears are misplaced. First, it is because de Certeau does not presume the prior existence of a reader in the form of a stable "I." Indeed, a question in "Reading as Poaching" destabilizes any attempt to situate reading as the activity of a fully formed subject existing independently: "*Who* reads in fact? Is it I, or some part of me?"[27]

Furthermore, de Certeau's anagnosological undertaking in fact aims to account for the reader as an *effect* (and not as a *cause*): the point is to clarify not only his "subjection" to power apparatuses, but also how he is fabricated, how he "constitutes (or 'edifies') himself as subject," what, using a Foucaldian vocabulary, we might call the reader's subjectivation. (De Certeau prefers to talk about "informing," in the sense of giving form to or "conforming.")[28]

This is the background for understanding what de Certeau, in "Reading as Poaching," calls "a politics of reading"[29] that plays out precisely at the tangential point where reading does not simply conform to what is written, but opens onto the possible exercise of a counterpower. Let us note that all kinds of texts and reading practices become "politicizable": the reader's experience, "oscillating...between what he invents and what changes him," is a "common experience" that obtains "no matter how popularized or technical" it is.[30]

There is therefore no reason to describe a reading as "authentic" or "real," as Heidegger or Blanchot do. Reading's emancipation is not limited to literature, to what Blanchot refers to as "the book whose origin is in art," as opposed to the "nonliterary" book, the reading of which, far from opening any sort of path, or inventing anything, would have always already taken place and could thereafter only reoccur in identical repetitions.[31]

Following de Certeau's anagnosology in adopting the principle that reading operations should be politicized, we will now turn to Hobbes's *Leviathan* (a "nonliterary book," if ever there was one) in order to examine the extraordinary and powerfully configuring connection that it weaves between a reading of politics and a politics of reading. As we will see, this is a machine that both reads and makes read in the most conforming and binding manner. At its core, however, under the name of "prophecy," we will detect a detachment that leads reading ahead of the text and ahead of itself.[32] Lurking at the heart of Leviathan, the monstrous machine, a sort of automaton destined to read (itself) imperturbably, absolute   or absolving — reading will turn out, in the end, to be a matter of speed. Or more precisely, it will appear to depend on a speed differential at the tangential point.

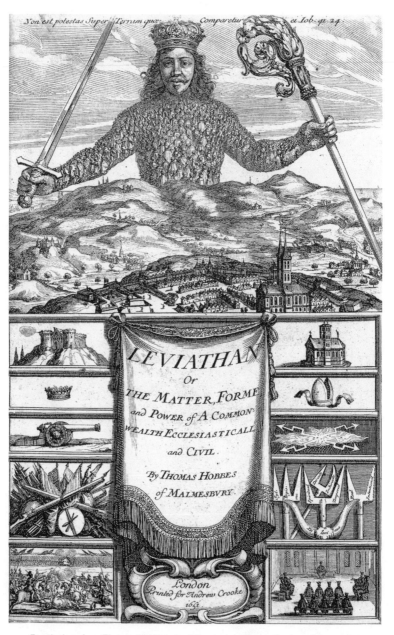

Frontispiece from Thomas Hobbes, *Leviathan*, engraving by Abraham Bosse, 1651

The Reading Machine

(*Leviathan*)

Open Hobbes's *Leviathan* and you are met by an image: the frontis-piece. In front of this temple, this monument erected to a certain conception of power, what awaits you, what faces or confronts you, is a headpiece and a head: the giant head of the sovereign. It stares straight out at you.

A symbol or an allegory (or a monstrous combination of those), this page requires reading as much as looking. Indeed, one can deci-pher a title that announces or promises what is hidden, setting that up at the remove that makes it an object of desire since the title appears on a curtain that hides the body of the text. Reading will be a matter of lifting the veil — the theater curtain — to fuse with what emerges on the other side.

Yet because the image itself is open to reading, reading already starts here, on this side of the wall hanging. To the left and to the right of the curtain, mirroring each other, we can make out the attributes of secular and ecclesiastical power: the fortress and the church, the crown and the miter, the cannons and the lightning bolts of excommunication, the weapons of battle and those of logic, military combat and theological debate (*disputatio*).

Carrying both these powers, holding a sword and a cross, the sovereign looks at me. His torso is composed of an accumulation of hundreds of men. Looks are exchanged between those men, him, and me. They cross paths in a pattern one might describe as the gaze of the people assembled in front of the sovereign "directed toward the giant's head and returns through his eyes back to the viewer," who adopts the "frog's perspective" of those who show only their backs "and, at the same time, is directly addressed" by the sovereign.[1] This composite image of a composite body thus assigns me, as a future reader, to a structurally double point of view.

On the one hand, it embeds me among the many figures whose backs are turned to me and whose gazes converge toward the sovereign: I am one of those subjects, one among all the others, subjected as are the others. On the other hand, however, it is I that the sovereign seems to be looking at, I and no one else: I am facing the sovereign in a sort of tête-à-tête that situates me outside the masses that compose his body.

Within the multitude and outside it, inside and outside: let us remember this divided position. Keep it in mind because it already tells us something about the place that will be ours as readers of this *Leviathan* on whose threshold we are poised.

As we cross over the threshold, entering through the introduction, we first encounter the famous characterization of the state as a monstrous automaton whose name is borrowed from the marine creature mentioned in the Bible:

> That great LEVIATHAN called a COMMONWEALTH, or STATE (in Latin, CIVITAS) which is but an artificial man; though of greater stature and strength than the natural, for whose protection and defence it was intended; and in which, the *sovereignty* is an artificial *soul*, as giving life and motion to the whole body; the *magistrates*, and other *officers* of judicature and execution, artificial *joints*.[2]

The description (the effiction)[3] of this great body politic continues as the other members and parts are mentioned. Its nerves (rewards and punishments), as well as its strength, its health and its disease (sedition), are briefly evoked, and the attention then turns to a motif that seems unrelated (is that why Hobbesian scholarship has so rarely noted it?), namely, the question of reading:[4]

> There is a saying much usurped of late, that *wisdom* is acquired, not by reading of *books*, but of *men*. Consequently whereunto, those persons, that for the most part can give no other proof of being wise, take great delight to show what they think they have read in men, by uncharitable censures of one another behind their backs. But there is another saying not of late understood, by which they might learn truly to read one another, if they would take the pains; and that is, *nosce teipsum, read thyself*; which was . . . meant . . . to teach us, that for the similitude of the thoughts, and the passions of one man, to the thoughts, and passions of another, whosoever looketh into himself . . . shall thereby read and know, what are the thoughts, and passions of all other men, upon the like occasions. . . . He that is to govern a whole nation, must read in himself, not this, or that particular man; but mankind: which though it be hard to do, harder than to learn any language, or science; yet, when I shall have set down my own reading orderly, and perspicuously, the pains left another, will be only to consider, if he also find not the same in himself. For this kind of doctrine admitteth no other demonstration.[5]

The *Leviathan*, this book whose threshold we have just crossed, thus presents itself as a *reading method*. Reading it will indeed be reading Hobbes's reading, a reading he has set down for us to make it easier for us to learn to read so that we may read one another, but also, and above all, so that we may learn to *read ourselves*, as advised by the deliberately erroneous translation of the precept that was inscribed on the front of the temple at Delphi and often attributed to Socrates: "Gnōthi seauton, nosce teipsum," or literally, "know yourself" rather than "read yourself."

To whom is this introduction addressed, as it presents the book to come as a political apprenticeship through reading? Who is the addressee of this reading of the political, mirrored, as we will see, by a politics of reading? It seems obvious that it is the sovereign himself ("He that is to govern a whole nation"). It is the *sovereign reader* whom *Leviathan* can help, sparing him some of the difficulty of reading.[6]

And yet *we* are the ones who are about to read it. Yes, we simple readers thus find ourselves in the double position to which the frontispiece assigned us. Our point of view as spectators had us oscillate between, on the one hand, participating in the multitude of the subjects' gazes and, on the other hand, being in a unique face-to-face with the sovereign. We begin to sense, and will have multiple chances of confirming, that in the same way, what we might call our reading posture makes us, on the one hand, a reader among so many others who are in the process of being subjected to a certain way of reading and, on the other hand, a sovereign reader called on to evaluate the validity of his reading every step of the way.

—◠

Let us then allow ourselves to be caught up and carried away by the workings of this reading machine, *Leviathan*. Reading it, we will be called on to submit to a certain reading regime, an anagnosological regime that the book builds at the same time as it constructs its theory about sovereignty and the state. To put it another way: over the course of our reading, we will construct ourselves as readers in exactly the way the space of the political is constructed.

What does this mean?

To get a clearer understanding, let us lend an ear to the way in which the question of reading returns, after the introduction, in a passage in the fourth chapter. Here, reading is described as a form of reasoning calculus, that is to say, as a patient exercise in reckoning [*capitaliser*] meaning, checking every step of the way. Hobbes contrasts what we might call accountant readers, who are capable of constantly producing accounts, with bad readers, the distracted readers who trust the written word far too much:

They which trust to books, do as they that cast up many little sums into a greater, without considering whether those little sums were rightly cast up or not; and at last finding the error visible, and not mistrusting their first grounds, know not which way to clear themselves; but spend time in fluttering over their books; as birds that entering by the chimney, and finding themselves enclosed in a chamber, flutter at the false light of a glass window, for want of wit to consider which way they came in.[7]

A reading worthy of the name, not a flighty, fickle reading, but a good reading, one that checks its own accuracy at every line, is thus essentially a calculating logic that regulates a monetary exchange of words. ("Words are wise men's counters, they do but reckon by them,"[8] says Hobbes in this same paragraph.) The accounting economy of reading is additive, cumulative: it proceeds from one sum to the next, it accrues (*capitalise*) names, verbs, phrases, chapters (*capitula*) in order to erect the structure of meaning.

Hobbes repeatedly asserts that everything — not just words — is open to such accumulation (*capitalization*): arithmeticians add numbers, geometers add lines and other figures, logicians do the same with phrases ("adding together two *names*, to make an *affirmation*; and two *affirmations*, to make a *syllogism*; and many *syllogisms* to make a *demonstration*").[9] This long list of all the domains in which calculations are made by adding also includes politics since "writers of politics, add together *pactions* [contracts] to find men's *duties*."[10] And just as this list — itself additive — of "all manner of things that can be added together"[11] is brought to a close, Hobbes concludes: "In sum, in what matter soever there is place for *addition* . . . there is also place for *reason*."[12]

In sum, yes, says Hobbes in the last sentence of this paragraph, wherever there are sums, that is to say, almost everywhere, one can proceed by addition as befits calculating reason. From arithmetic to politics, *in sum*, things work in the same way: you just need to substitute contracts for numbers. What Hobbes does not mention, however, is that the hold that addition has, spreading from one domain to the next, ever further, also takes over our reading at this very moment where we are reading. For how can we read these two words, *in sum*, which bring the demonstration concerning the reign of generalized addition to a close, unless by subscribing to it, miming, *in the very act of reading*, that movement of accumulation (*mouvement capitalisant*) that carries everything off with it? In sum, in reading *in sum*, we become those who sum.

And we increasingly become those who add, the more we read, the further we progress toward the final firework display, some forty chapters later. The general conclusion of *Leviathan* is indeed an apotheosis of *in sums*. It looks just like the sheet of calculations a treasurer might produce when checking his account book line by line. Here is what a mildly short-sighted or slightly nerdy accountant reader would see if he squinted only at the logical skeleton of the final chapter that summarizes the work: "I have showed before in the end of Chapter 21...In the 29th chapter, I have set down...In the 35th chapter, I have sufficiently declared...In the 36th chapter, I have said, that...And as to the whole doctrine...."[13]

After everything he has set out in the meantime about reason, power, the state, or religion, this summing, which is both exhilarating and a bit anxious, this grand finale of *in sums*, is a way for Hobbes to take leave of his readers: "I return," he confides, alluding to the drafting of his *De Corpore* (On the body), "I return to my interrupted speculation of bodies natural."[14] He sounds as though, after the laborious genesis of the Leviathan, the artificial body, he is doing his accounts on a Sunday and planning a holiday far from politics. In the meantime, however, he will have made us, his readers, swallow or incorporate a certain reading regime.

What happened?

From one sentence to another, one chapter to another, the *in sum* and all its look-alikes ("as I have shown," "I said that," etc.) count as or instantiate the partial addition that makes it possible, by reading, to pursue the accrual (*capitalisation*) all the way to the general sum, which is the conclusion. *In sum* — each time this little phrase appears, it functions as a representative for what came before it, a delegate for the part of the text that has been added and accumulated up to then.

In brief, *in sum* serves for our reading as the linguistic or syntactic equivalent of what Hobbes defines as a *person*: "He that acteth another, is said to bear his person, or act in his name...and is called in divers occasions, diversely; as a *representer*, or *representative*, a *lieutenant*, a *vicar*, an *attorney*, a *deputy*, a *procurator*, an *actor*, and the like."[15]

In sum, these two words that almost blend into a single word, are, for our reading, proxies that replace and represent what comes before them; they have a mandate to sum it up. Just as a pronoun is a noun's delegate, in this great calculation, in the sum of affirmations and syllogisms that Hobbes considers the reading of a discourse, all the forms of conjunction that indicate consequence are deputies that the text gives itself. They make it possible for the text to give itself the mandate to build itself up cumulatively. In this way, the reader literally becomes the spokesperson who carries the text forward, from one delegate to the next. *In sum*, the reader becomes the actor of the text's authority.

As the reading progresses from one sum to the next, the reader is erected as the *artificial person* that the text crafts at the same time as it erects its explicit object, the state. The result is that the automaton that is the Leviathan, whose construction is described by the book, faces another automaton that is also built one step at a time: the reader as a reading (adding) machine. On the one hand, we watch as the political edifice is erected by an accumulation of mandates for representation. ("A multitude of men, are made *one* person, when they are by one man, or one person, represented; so that it be done with the consent of every one of that multitude in particular,"[16] says Hobbes.) On the other hand, facing this Leviathan, who is thus also a person obtained through addition, there is the reader forged by the text, produced by adding partial sums that each represent multiple elements (words, phrases, chapters).

Each intermediary sum gathers elements, binding them in order to represent them, to be their deputies in the great sovereign assembly of meaning.

Leviathan marks the triumph of reading by binding. The reader shaped by this cumulative anagnosological regime has the task of finishing, through his reading, both the *Leviathan* text and the Leviathan state. Whereas the Leviathan is an *in sum* cumulated through the pyramidal verticality of political power, *Leviathan* (the book) is a horizontal, linear accretion that is the result of the binding power of reading.

This is the extraordinary entanglement that is knotted in the fabric of the text and toward which, one might say, both the frontispiece and the introduction already work: the aim is to interlace, to weave together, reading and politics, making the former into the *experience* of the latter. It is to work toward a *politics of reading*, in sum, a politics that is structurally inscribed in the very act of reading, whether or not the reader is aware of it. Thus, *Leviathan*, as a machine that forces one to read, is organized in exactly the same way as the governing machine. The conjunction of these two mechanisms, the analogy or homology of their regimes, their way of combining while operating together and simultaneously, make it possible for *Leviathan* to be set up as a great mechanism for *governing-reading*.

We have already charged through *Leviathan*'s conclusion, watching all the *in sums* light up each paragraph until they flicker into a grand pyrotechnic display of accumulation ("I have showed before ..."; "I have set down ..."; "I have sufficiently declared ..."; "I said that ..."). Yet this conclusion still holds a surprise for a closer reading. Indeed, at the culminating point of the additions, at the very point where ratiocinating accounting triumphs, *good* reading, reasonable and reasoning reading, the accounting reading that keeps track of everything it has read, becomes indistinguishable from *bad* reading, the flighty, distracted reading that, as you remember, was the reading of bird readers who fly over the pages.

Indeed, in the paragraph just before the final word (*finis*, in Latin), the reading regime that has been so patiently and laboriously constructed suddenly implodes:

> And as to the whole doctrine, I see not yet, but the principles of it are true and proper; and the ratiocination solid. For I ground the civil rights of sovereigns, and both the duty and liberty of subjects, upon the known natural inclinations of mankind, and upon the articles of the law of nature; of which no man, that pretends but reason enough to govern his private family, ought to be ignorant. And for the power ecclesiastical of the same sovereigns, I ground it on such texts, as are both evident in themselves, and consonant to the scope of the whole Scripture. And therefore am persuaded, that he that shall read it with a purpose only to be informed, shall be informed by it. But for those that by writing, or public discourse, or by their eminent actions, have already engaged themselves to the maintaining of contrary opinions, they will not be so easily satisfied. For in such cases, it is natural for men, at one and the same time, both to proceed in reading, and to lose their attention, in the search of objections to that they had read before.[17]

In sum, says Hobbes to the readers who have followed him up to this point, accepting his cumulative logic, we are of two sorts: either we simply want to be informed, or we must be convinced against our declared opinion.

Surely, those in the second category are best suited to serve as touchstones for *Leviathan*. Who could better embody the reading regime prescribed by the book than one who, never simply trusting the author, checks his reasoning step by step, double-checking all the intermediary sums in order to reach the total sum of the conclusion without errors? What better representative of the ratiocinating reading that Hobbes has constantly advocated than a pernickety reader who is never easily convinced, always objecting when there is a chance? Only such a reader could properly embody the figure of the *good reader* that was constructed throughout the text as a countermodel to the birds who whirl among pages to which they have given excessive trust.

However, the eminent reader, the reader who is distrustful enough to be meticulous, is also the reader *who does not read*. This is the reader who lets himself be distracted, the one who loses the thread as his attention turns toward possible objections. Indeed, if you listen carefully to this strange paragraph, you will hear Hobbes insisting that reading proceeds and stops *at the same time, simultaneously* ("it is natural for men, at one and the same time, both to proceed in reading, and to lose their attention"). Reading moves forward even as it is suspended. Or rather — and this is, in the end, the paradox of the cumulative regime in reading — *reading proceeds precisely insofar as it interrupts itself.*

In short, the good reading of *Leviathan* would, *in sum*, be a *permanent crisis* of its own continuity: at its hyperbolic point, at the apogee of its *overdrive*, reading as accruing threatens to implode; it becomes aporetic and stretched to breaking point: it delays what it anticipates as it moves backward. (Hobbes literally says that it moves forward in search of objections to what came before.)

At this point, we are wracked with infinite doubt. We don't quite know anymore what reading (according to) *Leviathan* means, nor can we clearly distinguish accountants from birds anymore.

Did we perhaps move too quickly, not checking our accounts each step of the way? Is there some passage we missed by skimming over too fast? Or did we, on the contrary, read too attentively to read well, object too much to be able to move forward?

Let us reread what we have already covered. Let us open once more this book we strode through with measured paces. Let us lend an ear, lingering or dawdling a little, to what might have already been resisting the conclusive apotheosis of the ratiocinating regime.

At the juncture between the second and third parts of *Leviathan*, at the beginning of chapter 32, we thus stumble on one of those apparently insignificant words or phrases that can, as we saw, turn out to be essential because it allows the text to fold onto itself, to make itself into its own delegate by inscribing a movement of accretion: "I have derived the rights of sovereign power, and the duty of the subjects *hitherto*, from the principles of nature only."[18]

We know now that what this *hitherto* nonchalantly prescribes, whether you like it or not, is a practice of reading as hoarding, adding what you read as you go. A reading that binds, thanks to gathering operators such as *hithertos* and other *in sums* that represent the text in the text and for the text. They are placeholders for what comes before; they are, as we said, like delegates or proxies for the text, which thus sends itself ahead of itself in order to build itself through accumulated delegations, through *mandates*.

Yet having thus reminded itself, in order to remind us, of what it has done, Hobbes's text announces, anticipates, what it will take on next. "In that I am next to handle," he declares, will be questions about a Christian commonwealth and Christian politics but also the divine word, notably when it becomes "prophetical."[19] *Leviathan* will thus consider prophecy and prophets, and these will be more than an extra theme in the book: they will inscribe the watermark of another reading regime. This will be a prophetic regime that, as we are about to see, definitely chooses the side of untying rather than gathering. (It is diastolic rather than systolic.)

What, according to Hobbes, is a prophet?

Let us read the triple definition in chapter 36, entitled "Of the Word of God, and of Prophets": "The name of prophet, signifieth in Scripture sometimes *prolocutor*; that is, he that speaketh from God to man, or from man to God: and sometimes *predictor*, or a foreteller of things to come: and sometimes one that speaketh incoherently, as men that are distracted."[20] The prophet, says Hobbes, is either *prolocutor* or *praedictor* (when he isn't simply *distracted*, or delirious). Depending on the meaning one wishes to assign to the prefix *pro-*, the pro-phet (from the Greek *phēmi*, "I say") is the one who speaks *in someone's stead* or *in advance*. Either, then, he lends his voice to proffer in another's stead (*pro-* in the sense of "for") or he will say in anticipation what is not yet (*pro-* in the sense of "pre-").

From the first to the second sense, prophecy, in Hobbes's eyes, loses value and authenticity; prophetic speech becomes an imposture, increasingly deprived of consistency or coherence as it detaches from the divine word, but also as it tends toward greater generality: "When by prophecy is meant prediction, or foretelling of future contingents; *not only* they were prophets, who were God's spokesmen, and foretold those things to others, which God had foretold to them; *but also* all those impostors, that pretend, by help of familiar spirits, or by superstitious divination of events past, from false causes, to foretell the like events in time to come."[21]

Not only the spokesmen, *but also* all manner of impostors: there are more and more prophets who use any available means, appeal to all sorts of causes, breaking down the connections between "false" causes and effects. There is no way of accounting for this disconnection of prophecy from all speech that carries authority. Prophecy leaves its legitimate and legitimated domain; it loses its composure or content to become nothing more than a particular way of relating to language in general. Without content, and therefore able to welcome any sort of event to come, prophecy becomes nothing more than the pure principle of disconnection between words: "And for incoherent speech, it was amongst the Gentiles taken for one sort of prophecy, because the prophets or their oracles, intoxicated with a spirit, or vapour from the cave of the Pythian oracle at Delphi, were for the time really mad, and spake like madmen; or whose loose words a sense might be made to fit any event."[22]

As it generalizes until it becomes merely one type of exchange through signs, prophecy becomes a sort of allegory of reading, and the prophet becomes the reader's double. Indeed, rereading this passage and reconsidering the three senses of the term "prophet," it starts to seem that our own way of reading is at stake here.

Is the reader not the one who, like a prophet, lends his voice and speaks for another, namely, for the text for which he is the *prolocutor* (as the actor would be the spokesperson for the character)? Is the reader not the one who, as he does this, is constantly anticipating, rushing toward what he has not yet read, toward what has not yet been written? Is the reader not the one who, thereby, through this very haste, becomes structurally distracted, that is, detached from the line of textual linearity, a reader thus facing *loose words* that nothing, no binding reason, gathers?

—☙

Let us continue to lend an ear to this prophetic regime of reading. It is this regime that, in line with an infernal rhythm of which Faust will be the name, will carry us toward the future of reading. It will carry us not only toward what awaits reading tomorrow (and already today), with the unheard-of development of techniques and anagnosological prostheses that are shaking up our experience as readers, but also and especially toward reading itself as a relation to the future, as a tension toward what is to come, beyond the text and beyond the reader, in the direction of a pure reading or an absolute reading that differs from the self.

Dear reader, do you feel as dizzy as I do? I am trying to remember when the solid ground, the stable bedrock of this apparently simple activity — reading — started to give way? The dual face to face of reading as one imagined it (a reader facing a text that he holds in his hands) became a threesome, and then a foursome. It gave way to a field of forces the effects of which can be discerned, tugging and pulling, even under the apparently smooth textual skin of *Leviathan*.

Leviathan's reader (meaning both the reader who reads the book and the reader who is constructed by the book) is the product of these underlying differential movements whose textual effects one can auscultate. As early as the introduction and throughout the book, there are echoes of the reading imperative that we have encountered so often. As you will remember, here it takes on the proverbial form of an old saying that cannot be attributed to anyone in particular and that enjoins us to read within ourselves: *read thyself.*

This self-reading, however, is itself modeled, chiseled out, by the reading of which the book is the trace or the inscription. ("When I shall have set down my own reading orderly, and perspicuously," says Hobbes, "the pains left another, will be only to consider, if he also find not the same in himself.") One reading thus informs another, one reader reads for another, who is shaped by and for the reading addressed to him.

We find here echoes of those complicated arrangements that Plato and Sade's anagnosological scenes taught us to notice: the sovereign reader and the subject reader, the accountant reader and the flighty reader, all inherit positions that were configured in the conflictual tensions between *erastai* and *erōmenoi*, or anagnosts and readees. Of course, the echoes are here slightly muted, dampened by the energy required to minimize the centrifugal tensions so as to preserve this regime of cumulative reading. Yet those tensions persist; they simmer under the surface. At the heart of this (teaching-) reading machine that is Hobbes's treatise, the dissension of those tensions produces the speed differential whereby the reading takes off from the text at the point at which the most concentrated and gathered reading attention — the most systolic — produces the greatest diastolic gap.

Either getting ahead of itself or tarrying behind itself, reading becomes tangential.

Fast Reading

(Three Times *Faust*)

A reader who rushes and guesses, a seer-reader who detaches himself from what is written and moves ahead of it—these are the figures that haunt Paul Valéry's notebooks. The notebooks contain many worried remarks on the matter: "The great problem for the modern writer is to ensure that he is read, i.e., to stop the reader from *guessing* the whole sentence or page,"[1] Valéry notes in 1915. The same term asserts itself in a fragment from the following year as a verb—"guessing instead of reading"[2]—and then in 1918–1919 as a noun:

> The evolution or modern literature is nothing more than the evolution of reading, which is tending to become a sort of guessing of *effects* by means of a few words, *seen* almost simultaneously, to the detriment of the pattern of the sentences.
>
> Advertisements and newspapers have led to *telegraphese* and a crude impressionism. People look, and no longer read.[3]

Valéry attributes this decline in reading to the atrophy of voice, upstaged by sight: "For centuries the human voice was the basis of literature.... The day came when people learned to read with their eyes, without spelling out, without listening to the sounds of the words and, as a result, literature was profoundly changed."[4] By thus giving up his voice—even an inner, tacit voice—by sacrificing it to the haste of saccadic eye movements, the reader would be on the verge of disappearing: "A close reader, reading slowly, with insight, taking his time, his mind open but alert . . . such readers, whose formation and variations would constitute the true subjects of the history of literature are dying out."[5]

In the era of Kindles and iPads that measure the speed and time of reading ("target reached," I saw flash on my screen after having read for half an hour), it is very tempting to accept Valéry's diagnosis at face value. And yet his nostalgia for a lost slowness is not specific to our modernity. It is actually one of the most, worn clichés, so often has it been repeated about reading.

We find it already in the first century AD, when Seneca recommends to Lucilius that he "digest" what he reads.[6] A thousand years later, the Cistercian monk William of Saint-Thierry advises in the same terms that one chew over carefully selected passages: "Some part of your daily reading [*de cotidiana lectione*] should also each day be committed to memory, taken in as it were into the stomach [*ventrum memoriae*], to be more carefully digested and brought up again for frequent rumination."[7]

If we jump blithely from one century to the next, like the rushed readers against whom these maxims and instructions warn us, we find similar claims all over the place: Schopenhauer asks of those who begin *The World as Will and Representation* that they be willing "*to read the book twice*, and to do so the first time with much patience."[8] Nietzsche, to whom Valéry so often refers, emphasizes the relevance of a slow pace for the reading of *Daybreak* ("I just as my book, are friends of *lento*")[9] and, indeed makes it the motto of the philologist that he is ("it is not for nothing that I have been a philologist, perhaps I am a philologist still, that is to say, a teacher of slow reading").[10]

While Valéry's criticism of speed reading is thus not particularly remarkable, it becomes striking when it is staged as a contemporary tragicomedy with universal implications. This is precisely what happens in his theatrical rewriting of the Faust legend, where

Valéry makes the pact with the devil and the desire for infinite appropriations into a truly anagnosological drama, a drama of reading in the era of what Goethe was the first to call "world literature" (*Weltliteratur*).

Certain passages of *"My Faust"*—for such is the title of this modern version of the Faustian legend—seem even to anticipate the becoming electronic of reading, as we now experience it on our screens. At the moment he signs the fateful contract with Mephistopheles, the hero declares: "Deeds and signatures are finished with. Today the written word flies faster than the spoken, and the spoken flies carried by light."[11]

To understand how far the Faustian reading gets caught up in unheard-of acceleration in the era of hypertext, we need briefly to recall the two tragedies by Goethe that already evoke the act of reading, explicitly or allegorically.

As early as the prologue of *Faust I*, the theater director says of the spectators (those doubles for us, the readers) who have taken their seats to watch the tragedy: "They've done an awful lot of reading" (*sie haben schrecklich viel gelesen*).[12] Their (our) reading is thus qualified in anticipation as extensive rather than intensive. As for Faust (that other doppelgänger for the readers that we are), his reading is marked by the theme of flight when, in the long nocturnal monologue that immediately follows the celestial prologue, he calls out to the moon:

> O radiant moon for whom I have
> so often, waking at this desk,
> sat at midnight watching until
> I saw you, melancholy friend, appear
> above my books and papers—would that this
> were the last time you gazed upon my grief!
> If only I, in your kind radiance,
> could wander in the highest hills
> and with spirits haunt [*schweben:* float around] some mountain cave,
> could rove the meadows in your muted light.[13]

Faust seems to dream of reading by taking off from the myopic proximity of the lines on the page, looking at piled-up writings from on high, espousing a flyover movement in which contemporary theorists of *distant reading* might recognize themselves.[14]

We know that Goethe was a passionate enthusiast for the first attempts at hot-air balloon flight. And his Faust, in the first part of his tragedy, does not simply dream of flying, he actually does fly and flies well: "We'll simply lay my cloak out flat; / it will carry us through the air,"[15] Mephistopheles tells him, explaining that a little "heated air" (*Feuerluft*) will help them lift off the earth.

In *Faust II*, the theme of air travel and the view from above is tied in with the surprising figure of the *homunculus*, which appears in act 2 to produce a masterful allegory of reading, one that anticipates the era of Google and the World Wide Web. The little artificial man, who is issued not from "old-fashioned procreation," but "by mixing many hundred substances,"[16] accompanies Mephistopheles and a sleeping Faust on the balloon trip that takes them all the way to Classical Walpurgisnight, flying over centuries and centuries of universal literature on the way.

Floating in the air with Faust and Mephistopheles, gliding a bit above them, this humanoid is like an aerostatic bedside light: "What is that unexpected meteor / Its shining light reveals a solid sphere,"[17] exclaims Erichtho, the magician, when she sees this strange nightlight or reading light in the shape of a homunculus looking at her from above. And we understand the surprise of this literary character, mentioned by both Ovid and Dante. We understand how baffled Erichtho must have been, from her point of view, which seems to be at ground level (or, better, at the level of the text she inhabits), when she sees an improbable reading arrangement reading her from on high.

In this scene, which is even more fantastical than the others, the *homunculus* is like a ray of light that scans the entire belles-lettres archive. ("I shall explore the world a bit [*ein Stückchen Welt*],"[18] he says.)

Keeping in mind these Faustian reading scenes and what they already suggest on the subject of reading speed in the era of world literature, let us now turn to the third Faust, Valéry's Faust.[19]

Before even knowing anything about what awaits me in the "sketches" that Valéry collected under the peculiar title *"My Faust,"* I can already assert that like countless other readers before me, I would like to be able to use that phrase. I would like to be able at to least pronounce it to myself, for it is the formula that attests to a reading worthy of the name. To say "my Faust" is to sign as a reader, whether my reading is simply one among many other readings or it is a fabulous reinvention.

Yet facing Valéry's title, I am immediately and radically dispossessed of the possibility of appropriation that animates all reading. If I were to say "my Faust," I would only be quoting his move. (If I declared Faust "mine," at that very moment, the way it would have of "being mine" would be to be his.) Furthermore and above all, appropriation seems impossible because the quotation marks with which Valéry grips his catch immediately mark that it is not his:[20] "My Faust," he seems to say, is "'mine'" only in a manner of speaking.

Hence, then, it is as though he were predicting to each future Faustian reader that Faust will be theirs only in a false sense — that they might, then, want to get rid of him. Sure, I'll pass him on to you, he seems to say to us, that Faust who has a diabolical way of dropping you as soon as you consider him yours. On the threshold of his *"My Faust,"* simply reading the title, we can sense that we are already bound to experience a radical expropriation: his *"My Faust"* will never really become my "My Faust."

The preface is just as striking and unsettling. In his address "to the reader of good faith and bad will" (*au lecteur de bonne foi et de mauvaise volonté*),[21] one can hear whispers of a whole series of earlier addresses. Montaigne's, for instance, who, with this warning at the front of his *Essays* — "Reader, you have here a book whose faith can be trusted" — moved as if immediately to dismiss him: "Therefore, Reader, I myself am the subject of my book: it is not reasonable that you should employ your leisure on a topic so frivolous and vain. Therefore, Farewell."[22] Capturing the reader's good will, asking him for his trust, and then immediately dismissing him: here, too, there is a move in which appropriation and expropriation are inextricably combined.

A similar thing happens in Baudelaire in the inaugural poem from *The Flowers of Evil*, where the famous final apostrophe ("Hypocrite reader, — fellowman, — my twin!" (*Hypocrite lecteur, — mon semblable, — mon frère!*)[23] combines both complicit identification and falseness in a single contradictory injunction. Valéry in fact no doubt had the Baudelairian address in mind, not only because he explicitly inverts its sign (hypocrisy becomes "good faith"), but also and especially because, further in the play (act 3, scene 7), he will reprise it in a quasi-citation that knowingly operates a gender switch, when Faust's Student says to his "secretary," Lust, as she is called: "You are my kind . . . my sister" (*vous, ma semblable, ma sœur*).[24] We will soon have to lend an ear to this female reader who mirrors the Baudelairian reader and who also announces Calvino's Other Reader.

Still, the preface of *"My Faust,"* which thus borrows its manner of addressing the reader from others, is mostly occupied with justifying the appropriation of Goethe's dramatic poem by arguing that Faust and Mephistopheles, as characters, never in fact belonged to their author:

> The personality of Faust, like that of his fearful partner, has an indefinite right to fresh reincarnations. It might seem as if the act of genius which first redeemed these two from their state of puppetry, in legend or sideshow, and raised them . . . to the highest degree of poetic being, must prevent any other inventive imagination from ever again taking their names, reanimating them. . . . However there is no surer index of creative power than the

creature's refusal to submit or remain constant to his creator's intentions. The greater the creature's life, the greater his freedom . . . . That is why I have been bold enough to make my own use of them."[5]

And Valéry goes on to say that using these characters is to imagine "an indefinite number of works": "Melodramas, comedies, tragedies, pantomimes, according to the occasion; in verse or prose, as mood might require." In other words, he imagines an infinite text, infinitely destined to being unfinished, as attested by the status of "sketches" attributed to the parts that compose this third *Faust*.

"*My Faust*" will be precisely a drama in which Faust escapes himself, disseminating himself in a hypertext without borders that condemns him — and condemns us, his readers — to experience something that cannot be appropriated. For in this third segment of his textual existence (which is also necessarily the last, as we will see), Faust writes. He is a writer, the author of his own legend, as he explains to a Mephistopheles, who appears widely discredited — "your reputation in the world isn't quite so grand as it used to be"[26] — over the course of an extraordinary dialogue in which what is clearly at stake is our status, the status of the readers:

> FAUST: Listen: I want to create a great work, a book. . . .
>
> MEPHISTO: You? Aren't you satisfied with *being* a book?
>
> FAUST: I have special reasons for this one. I want it to be an inextricable blend of my true and my false memories, my ideas, my intuitions, my well-conducted hypotheses and deductions, my experiments with the imagination: all my many voices in one! A book one could begin at any point and leave off at any other. . . .
>
> MEPHISTO: Nothing very new there. Any reader will do that for you.
>
> FAUST: Maybe no one will read it; but anyone who does will never be able to read another.
>
> MEPHISTO: He'll be dead of boredom. . . .
>
> FAUST: . . . I have this great work in mind. I want it to rid me finally of myself, of the self from which I already feel so detached.[27]

Faust's book, the work in which he would tell all about himself so thoroughly that he could finally say (to himself): I am mine, I am "my Faust," that book would also be the one that would make it impossible for Faust to coincide with himself ("this great work ... I want it to rid me finally of myself"). This *"My Faust"* would be the masterpiece of each reader ("any reader will do that"), as long as it became indifferent to all reading ("a book one could begin at any point and leave off at any other"). In short, this book of all Fausts would be the book of books, the hyperbook in which reading would be forever locked up ("anyone who does [read it] will never be able to read another"), but it would be worth nothing to that reader ("anyone [who] does" will be "dead of boredom").

The hyper-Faust—his hypertext that includes all the others ("all my many voices in one!")—could not be read anymore. Not because it is inaccessible and unreadable but because it is hermetic. Rather, paradoxically, because it could only be read and reread incessantly, because there would be nothing else to read than this Faustian hyperarchive; no reading of it could catch a glimpse of its edges.

This tragedy of reading in the era of the Faustian hypertext is not just the subject or the theme of *"My Faust,"* the book we are reading. By reading it, we are in the process of living through what the readers in the book experience since for us, as for them, it is impossible to decide where the text begins and where it ends. We just read what we thought was its preface (it was addressed to us with a reassuring anti-Baudelairian wink to trust and faith); we now find ourselves facing these same words, this time *in* the text that Faust has just dictated and that we reread just as Lust reads them to him:

LUST (*reads*): "To the reader of good faith and bad will ... "
FAUST: That's the ideal reader.... I shall put this into Latin.... Go on...
LUST (*reads*): "So much has been written about me that I no longer know who I am. True, I have not read all the many works....[28]

The preface's address, outside the book, has been swallowed into the hyper-Faust, of which it is no longer simply the preface.

This book, which no longer has a clearly defined outside, is thus, also the hyperbook in which we, the readers, are locked. And in which, as Mephisto says, we are bored to death. For boredom is no doubt one of the affects most characteristic of this world literature that Goethe names and theorizes,[29] whereas Valéry's Faust seems to predict its becoming hypertextual. (Remember, he already refers to writings that fly "carried by light.") Faust himself is the first to be bored — understandably — because he is henceforth only an eternal return of himself and, by definition, nothing new can happen. Hyper-Faust sinks into a hyperboredom; understanding himself ahead of time, he is bored to death:

> I made the real voyage round the real world.... Then, still under the guidance of my fate, I came back into time.... To live again. As I am now. I am living, seeing, knowing again, if it is the same thing to do the same thing again.... The boldest, the most unprecedented idea that occurs to me cannot ever seem new to me. The moment it occurs, I feel that I have thought and rethought it before.[30]

In other words, Faust suffers from what Valéry, in his *Notebooks*, called "cyclosis" or "cyclomania."[31]

Faust, however, is not the only one to be bored. His Student also succumbs to this evil that corrodes everything, and he ends up falling asleep in the master's library with "walls lined with books."[32] You can imagine him, snoring lightly, "asleep, pillowed on an open folio," as two devils strike up a dark hymn to general boredom:

> ASHTAROTH: I'm bored, bored, bored.... Oh! How bored I am!...Krek, krek.... Gnaw, scrape, file, crunch.... Everything bores, and boredom bores and bores me.... Krek, krek....
> BELIAL: Scrunch, scrunch.... What is it you're gnawing at?
> ASHTAROTH: Everything.... Hearts, bodies, reputations, populations... and the rocks!... Time even.... I grind to ash.... Krek, krek....[33]

When four scenes later the Student wakes up, one might for a moment think that he fell asleep because he dove too deep into the texts instead of skimming over them:

STUDENT: Ah-aagh.... (*Yawns.*) What a lot of books.... I've never read so ma-a-a-ny.... Oo-oof....

MEPHISTO: ... You were reading a bit too close, with your nose glued to that sticky prose.

STUDENT: My nose?.... Well, after all, reading's a matter of keeping your nose on the move. First it travels to the right, and then it jumps back to the left and begins again.[34]

Does it turn out that careful reading with attention to detail is soporific? Might Anglo-Saxon close reading or French *explication de texte* be the cause of the Student's narcosis?[35] We need only look at ourselves for a moment, we Faustian readers from the hypertextual era, to see that Mephisto's explanation does not hold: whereas we may speed up reading, devour books, or even just guess at them, consuming ever more, boredom will no doubt only increase.

Reader, are you still there? Are you asleep? Are you still willing to follow me?

The only one who seems to keep a desire to read almost intact in *"My Faust"* is Lust, whose name in English of course means desire or craving, whereas in German, it also signifies "pleasure" and "volup-tuousness." The best interpreters of *"My Faust"* have quite rightly heard those resonances,[36] but they forget another possibility that if one is attentive to the anagnosological dimension of Valéry's version of the Faustian tragedy must prevail, namely, that *lust* is an old spelling for the French verb *lire* ("to read") in the third person of the imperfect subjunctive.

Here is one among many examples, chosen because it is about reading: Louis Sébastien Le Nain de Tillemont, a Church historian, describes how Pope Damasus I, who had entrusted Saint Jerome with the task of preparing a new Latin translation of the Bible, worried that the latter "read more than he wrote" (*lisoit plus qu'il n'écrivoit*) and then added: "Damasus did not disapprove of the fact that he read, but he wanted those readings to produce the fruit proper to them, that is to say books" (*Damase ne desapprouvoit pas qu'il lust; mais il vouloit que ses lectures produisissent le fruit qui leur est propre, c'est à dire des livres*).[37]

It may seem strange to suggest that Lust embodies the subjunctive mood of reading, given that on the one hand, her name is often followed by a stage direction in the indicative mood asserting that "she reads" and, on the other hand, it is often preceded by an imperative as Faust orders her to read what she has written under his dictation. Consider, for instance, this passage: "Faust: Well then, read over the beginning. Lust (*She takes up a notebook and reads*)." Or again, three times in a row: "Faust: ... Go on. Lust (*reads*)."[38]

Yet it is precisely as though Lust's name, caught between the imperative to read ("Go on," "Read again") and the indicative mood of a reading that actually takes place ("she reads"), holds onto something about reading that cannot be contained either in the instant of reading or in its programmed execution.

—☙

How, then, does Lust read? Are we even sure that she does read?

Remember those semblances of reading to which Lacan referred in his seminar, when we dream that we read or mime reading (maybe because we don't know how to read), or when we already know the text by heart. Well, when Lust is in the position of an anagnost or an *erōmenos*, when she lends her voice to the text she writes down for Faust, she, too, might only appear to be reading. Indeed, she ends up admitting to the one she calls "my Master" that "I can only confess that I scarcely listen to what I read back to you.... And when you are dictating, my mind is always on something else, even while I am writing."[39]

The distracted Lust would no doubt have a hard time answering Lacan's question, "When are you sure that you are reading?" She is, of course, the one to whom Faust's reading imperative is addressed. She does, of course, execute his orders. Yet it nevertheless seems impossible to be certain that she actually reads; her reading remains hypothetical, impossible to determine.

According to the definition traditionally given by grammarians, this uncertainty is precisely one of the characteristics of the subjunctive (the other characteristic being subordination). For instance, in the article on conjugation in Diderot and d'Alembert's *Encyclopedia*, César Chesneau Dumarsais writes, "the subjunctive expresses an action in a way that is dependent, subordinate, uncertain and conditional."[40] To say that Lust embodies reading in the subjunctive (she of whom Faust wanted that she read [*qu'elle lût*]) is thus to say that her reading is conjectural (one can only suppose or desire it) and derivative (with respect to the indicative of what is, namely, the Faustian text).

By being elusive (because it is never certain), does Lust's reading not thwart the submission that would seem to be its lot? Lust is clearly Faust's *erōmenos* and plays the role of the anagnost who responds to his imperative, and yet she remains elusive; she does not let herself be entirely possessed by this *erastēs* who is also her readee. (He asks her to read to him what he himself has written.) Indeed, Lust, reading subjunctively, is impossible to locate, even as she is there, apparently present; she is elsewhere, not even listening to what she reads and is thus what, in reading, *leaves something wanting*; she is what is not captured in the actuality of reading.

Lust's name and the subjunctive whose optative value she embodies (the aspiration, the wish, or the fervor to read) thus seem to indicate the source of a certain inspiration to resist the subjugation inherent in reading, an impetus toward what is to come.[41] In Lust, the speed differential that constitutes reading — one voice dropping behind or overtaking another one — does not seem to lead to the Faustian vision of a general acceleration ending in exhaustion and boredom. In her, the gap between voices that are reading and those that are read gestures instead toward what might be a loophole, an improbable and ephemeral fissure in the hyperarchive, a loophole that offers a glimpse of what propels and moves reading, namely, to use the phrase Benjamin borrows from Hofmannsthal, "reading what has never been written."

We must ponder this phrase, a variation on one that we had already encountered in Blanchot. We will have several occasions to return to it. We must listen carefully in order to try to hear what it announces. It does not speak of the illegible in the sense of the indecipherable. (What is not written is not yet hermetic.) Neither does it refer to the unreadable in the hypertextual sense of the too much to read (what makes the Student exclaim, as he wakes up in the middle of the Faustian bookshelf caving under the weight of the books: "All this to raise inch by inch, century by century, a monument of the UNREADABLE.")[42] Instead, it names what filters out, like a ray of light, through the very phrasing of a reading that is *tangentially* engaged in the text.

What is it that filters out in this way?

To understand that, we must now turn to a certain Korin, a post-Faustian character in so many ways, and follow him in his extraordinary quest.

Cher lecteur solitaire, fatigué, sensible, je t'invite à
glisser cette lettre dans l'encoche du livre que tu trou-
veras en librairie le 23 octobre 2013. Tu sais pourquoi.

László Krasznahorkai

DÉP. LÉG. OCT. 2013
ISBN 978-2-36624-002-3
6 euros TTC France
www.cambourakis.com

László Krasznahorkai, *La Venue d'Isaïe*, trans. Joëlle Dufeuilly (Paris: Cambourakis, 2013)

Readers' Correspondence

(*War and War*)

A singular address introduces the reader to the French translation of
László Krasznahorkai's brief piece, "Isaiah Has Come." This address
should be given a unique place in a long series in which we would
find the "idle reader" (*desocupado lector*) from the prologue to *Don
Quixote*, the "hypocrite reader" from the first poem in *The Flowers
of Evil*, and the "reader of good faith and bad will" from *"My Faust."*
Here, I, the reader, am addressed as follows: "Dear solitary, tired
sensitive reader, I invite you to slip this letter into the slit in the book
you will find in bookstores on October 23, 2013. You know why."

These lines are printed on the back flap of a cover that looks like
an envelope.[1] The reader who is addressed in this manner is asked to
insert this narrative, sealed as a letter would be, into the back cover
of another volume by the same author, *War and War*, the great novel
that "Isaiah Has Come" announces. We, who are preparing to read,
thus are first called on to perform a postal operation involving the
insertion of one book into a slit in another, as though into a textual
mailbox where, thanks to the mailmen that we are, one writing
reaches another, its addressee.

Reading would then, first and foremost, involve participating in
the postal work of a readers' correspondence (*courrier des lecteurs*).[2]
The missives involved are not letters sent, for instance, by readers
to their newspaper in order to share their opinions, reactions, or

questions. Nor is this a reference to places where such missives are printed, such as advice columns or letters to the editor. Here, it is a matter of an envelope *entrusted to the readers* for them to convey it somewhere. What is at stake in this readers' correspondence is *the readers themselves as couriers*, as the messengers carrying the dispatch they were handed.

Krasznahorkai implicitly equates such a task for reading with prophecy. Indeed, the narrative that accompanies the address that we read, this narrative that assigns a postal mission to the reader, carries the name of a biblical prophet: Isaiah. Not that we will know in any way exactly how he is related to the pages bearing the title "Isaiah Has Come," since there is no mention of Isaiah himself in them. What the pages tell, without ever mentioning Isaiah (who thus remains confined to the threshold of the title), is instead the story of György Korin, the main character, who has washed up, dead drunk, at the buffet of a bus station in an indeterminate place.

We will encounter Korin again in the novel, *War and War*, of which "Isaiah Has Come" is just a forerunner. Is he a prophet? And if so, why, and of what?

In a tautological or autoprophetic way, Korin is first and foremost the prophet of his own recurrence. Since we find him in both books, the prophecy seems to concern the very return of the protagonist: the prediction of a work to be published comes true with the successful delivery of the missive carried by the readers when they insert the story into the slit in the back cover of the novel, where it was expected.

The text of *War and War*, in fact, implicitly remembers the end of "Isaiah Has Come" in that it recalls the bullet that transpierces Korin's hand in the last pages: "An *old thing*, he said in English, not interesting…a very long time ago, at a time when he had felt bitterly disappointed, and he was almost embarrassed to mention it now for the whole disappointment was so childish, but what happened was that he had shot through it."[3] And of this scar, this stigma, Korin would "carry the mark around for the rest of his life,"[4] like an indelible slit on the body or the corpus of the textual being that he is.

Korin is not, however, only a prophet because he announces himself, promises his character's recurrence from "Isaiah Has Come" to *War and War*. He is also a prophet insofar as, as we read in Hobbes, any prophet is both a *prolocutor* who speaks *for* and a *praedictor* who says *ahead of time*. Hobbes, you may remember, added a third possible meaning of the term, a more trivial sense, with no apparent connection to the first two: a prophet is the one who "speaketh incoherently," so that from his "loose words" one can infer a signification that "might be made to fit any event."

At first glance, it would seem that Korin is only a prophet in this third sense (but we will patiently let the other two senses emerge). When, in "Isaiah Has Come," he tells the man beside him at the bar, who lights one cigarette after another, inhaling deeply, that the general project of ruin and degradation of the world is "horribly successful,"[5] his way of articulating the word "horribly" (*iszonytatóan*) pushes his diction to the limits of language:

> Horribly, in his opinion, he repeated, and, for the sake of emphasis lingered as long as he could on the word "horribly," which so slowed his speech that he almost came to a stop near the end of it, a remarkable achievement since all the way through, right from the beginning, he had been speaking as slowly and with as little passion as it was possible to speak, every syllable reduced to its mere phonemes, as if each of them were the product of a struggle against other syllables or phonemes that might have been uttered in its place, as though some kind of deep and complex war were being fought out somewhere at the bottom of his throat, in which the right syllable or phoneme had to be discovered, isolated, and torn from the clutches of the superfluous ones, from the thick soup of syllable-larvae energetically thrashing about there then carried up the throat, led gently through the dome of the mouth, forced up against the row of teeth and finally spat forth into freedom, into the terminally stale air of the buffet, as the only sound apart from the sick, continuous moaning of the refrigerator, a sound heard on the edge of the bar where the man was standing immobile; hor-rib-ly

[*i-szony-ta-tó-an*], in his opinion, Korin said, slowing, after which he did not so much hesitate as come to a complete stop.[6]

Phonation thus emerges from a "war" (*csata*) that precedes elocution. We will have to wonder whether that is the war to which the title *War and War* refers, namely, a war that seems to have no opposite, no peace that could counter it, a war that, like Krasznahorkai's sentences, constantly puts off its final stop. Indeed, there are variations in intensity, relative truces, but there is never an end.[7]

Further on in "Isaiah Has Come," a countermovement to the disaggregation of syllables ("hor-rib-ly") appears in Korin's troubled elocution. This countermovement is just as destabilizing since this time, the syllables "ran into each other," they collided, and "it was like watching a train crash, the engine hitting the stationary vehicle."[8] The "revolution" (*fordulat*) Korin wants to talk about with his silent barmate thus becomes a "rvshon" (*frlat*) and its "world-historical" (*világtörténelmi*) scale condenses to "wrldstical" (*vlágtrömm*).[9]

It is in this mode of crush, or crasis[10] that Korin, a contemporary Isaiah, looks toward the future: "I...lkdnto...the-fyoor...atard...spisl...," he mumbles, which the narrator translates to "I looked into the future at our disposal."[11] Korin's prophetic words are thus not only detached words, loosened like the loose words Hobbes attributes to prophets speaking incoherently, they are also words that are squashed against one another, crushed, with no intervals between them.

This is neither the first nor the last time that Krasznahorkai resorts to compressed writing. Before "Isaiah Has Come," in *Satantango*, his first novel published in 1985, he transcribed the dreams of villagers sleeping in a huge uninhabited house by giving up not only periods and commas but even some of the blank spaces between words: "Mrs. Schmidt was a bird happily flying through the milk of theclouds seeing someonedownthere wavingather soshedes cendeda littleland could hear."[12]

The author notes these dreams, dreams that rise like a swirling and captivating vapor above the sleeping little collective, using something like the ancient practice of *scriptio continua*, found on the manuscript scrolls on which texts — Plato's, for instance — were written without any spacing between the different elements of the sentence.

More recently, in 2010, Krasznahorkai wrote a story to go with images by Max Neumann, a German artist. *Animalinside*: the absence of any spacing between the words in the title — as though prefiguring a limitless expansion, one that would leave no blanks — announces the potentially infinite growth of the first-person narrator, a force, no doubt, a blind power enclosed somewhere inside:

> So big am I that I extend from the top of one tree to another, I extend from one church spire to another, I extend from one village to another, I extend from one city to another, I extend from one country to another, and if I want I extend from one continent to another, and if I want I extend all the way across the Atlantic Ocean, and if I want I extend all the way across the Pacific Ocean, I extend from the Amazon to the islands of Japan, I extend from the North Pole to the South Pole.[13]

It is unclear who says "I" here. And the indication that the title seems to give — one imagines a chained animal looking for escape — is quickly belied ("because I am not an animal, and I am not a specter, and not a shadow").[14] Maybe it is the sentence that, as it says "I" in this way, describes its infinite expansion? The world sentence, the universe sentence, is certainly one of the most constant temptations in Krasznahorkai's writing. We will come back to this.

As we were saying, Korin's elocution, his diction, has a prophetic tone. His speech and his enunciation oscillate between disaggregation and compression. But how is his discourse that of a prophet in the two other senses Hobbes gives to the term, that of a *prolocutor* and a *praedictor*?

In "Isaiah Has Come," we don't yet know anything about what Korin was doing before the first pages, that is, before he "applied the brakes by the entrance to the NON STOP buffet at the bus station."[15] In *War and War*, on the other hand, we learn early on that he is an "archivist" and even that he is "head-archivist-in-waiting."[16] It is in the archive, "some two hundred kilometers southwest of Budapest,"[17] among the shelves laden with documents, that one fine day he discovers the "manuscript" of which he will later say that it contains "the most extraordinary piece of writing that anyone had ever produced."[18]

This encounter, after which Korin the archivist becomes first and foremost a reader, marks a turning point in the narrative. One day,

> vaguely checking the shelves, as he put it, utterly by chance, he arrived at a shelf he had never before explored, took down from a box that had never been taken down, not at least since the Second World War, that was for sure, and from this box labeled "Family Papers of no Particular Significance" took out a fascicule headed IV.3/1941-42, opened it and, in doing so, his life changed forever.[19]

This turning point, this upheaval, situates reading — the act of reading — at the heart of the narrative. We will reread its telling — twice, in fact — as told by Korin himself to the Hungarian interpreter who puts him up in New York, Mr. Sárváry. At that point, we learn a little more about the manuscript itself, and we follow, step by step, page by page, hour after hour, Korin's reading of it, the reading of the first reader:

> At first [he] just looked at it as a whole, casually leafing through, to and fro, observing the year of entry, picking out names of individuals . . . though this proved fruitless since the one hundred and fifty to one hundred and eighty pages, or so he calculated, carried no accompanying note, no name, no date, no clue in the form of a postscript as to who had written it or where, in fact not a thing, nothing . . . so what on earth is it . . . he realized it required

a different approach, so he actually decided to read the text . . . sat and read while the clock above the entrance showed first five, then six, then seven, and while he did not once look up, proceeding to eight, nine, ten, eleven o'clock already, and still he sat in exactly the same place in exactly the same way, until he did glance up and saw that it was seven minutes past eleven, even remarking loudly on the fact, saying, what the heck, eleven-o-seven already, then quickly packing the things away . . . still holding the package, turning off the lights and locking the glazed entrance door behind him with the idea that he would continue his reading at home, starting all over from the beginning.[20]

If it had gone on like that, if the narrative had continued to chronograph the pure passage of time spent reading ("five, then six, then seven . . . "), we would have ended up simply reading Korin as he reads, reading him read or reading him reading, he who moves from the skimming reading of an archivist to a careful reading worthy of the name. Having been a prophet with a perturbed diction (disaggregated or compressed) in "Isaiah Has Come," in *War and War*, Korin thus becomes a representative for us as we read him. He is therefore a prolocutor in Hobbes's sense for more than one reason: he speaks *for* the text (he reads it in manuscript, he lends his silent anagnost's voice to the text so that it may be heard), and he does this *for* the readers that we are (his reading is destined for us, we the readees who welcome it).

Korin thus reads and rereads the extraordinary manuscript that he discovered in the archives where he worked. He has now left that obscure place somewhere south of Budapest to carry his discovery, to transport it, as a courier for the readers that we are, to New York, to take it in person to what he describes several times as the "center of the world."[21] Korin, the mailman or carrier of words who is working for us, goes to that city, whose "references to Babel"[22] he eventually understands, in order to deliver the manuscript to posterity. Or rather, to deliver it to what he first calls "immortality,"[23] later, correcting himself, "a momentary isle of eternity," namely, "among the millions of pieces of information stored by computers" in the "virtual realm" of memory called the internet.[24]

Korin the courier does not stop there, however. Having detected in the "eternal" internet a space that might escape the destruction that threatens "the various repositories...books, scrolls, films, microfiches, encryptions, engravings and so forth,"[25] having successfully completed the "task he had set himself," namely, "to pass on that which, if it didn't sound too portentous to put it like this, had been bestowed on him,"[26] in short, after having transcribed and uploaded online the entire text of the manuscript that he decided to call *War and War* in English,[27] Korin realizes that the real challenge is just beginning: the ultimate task for him to accomplish would be to find "a way out."[28]

What kind of exit are we talking about? From where, whereto?

In order to understand this, we must delve further into the manuscript that Korin keeps reading and rereading so that we may meet four characters. The text offers a description of their intermittent appearances and characteristics: "Kasser delicate and thoughtful, Falke gentle and bitter, Bengazza tired and secretive, Toót harsh and distant, faces and expressions you see once and never forget."[29] These four appear out of nowhere with no warning, each time in a different context: ancient Crete, mid-nineteenth-century Cologne (as the construction of the cathedral picks up again), Venice in 1423, before the election of Francesco Foscari as doge, Gibraltar on the eve of Christopher Columbus's return, on Hadrian's Wall at the edges of the Roman Empire. They arrive just when everything is about to tip into war. And each time, a fifth character, the obscure Mastemann, is somehow the vector, the ferment, or the emblem of destruction.

What Kasser, Falke, Bengazza, and Toót seek is peace, "the most complete peace yet known,"[30] the peace of which Kant said "to attach the adjective 'perpetual' to it is already suspiciously close to a pleonasm," for a peace that is not definitive is just a truce, a temporary suspension of hostilities.[31] As for the sinister Mastemann, he constantly brings war or sings its praises and in the end always squashes the four pacifists' hopes.

We can now better understand why Korin ends up choosing *War and War* as the title for the manuscript that he transcribes and uploads on the internet. Contrary to Leo Tolstoy's famous novel to which it alludes, contrary also to what the four protagonists of the narrative in the narrative would like to think, this title seems to say that there is no opposite of war.

Is that what Korin rereads in the text over and over again? That there is only war and war, degrees of war, and that war never really has an opposite or an antonym worthy of the name? Perhaps. However, for we who read Korin reading, it is as though an extra layer were added, complicating the title. For we wonder: What is a perpetual war — war and war and war… — *in reading*?

In a certain sense, this is already Korin's question when he gets around to looking for the famous "way out." The author of the manuscript had looked for one for the four characters he had invented, Kasser, Falke, Bengazza, and Toót. After having sent them into the "realm of history, into the reality of eternal war," he had tried to "settle them at a point that held the promise of peace," but had failed because "there is only war and war."[32]

Korin seems to take up this failed irenicism from the manuscript's author, absorbing it or incorporating it, he who is now in charge of the four characters, he who is now their courier, as it were, he who, reading them, "walks up and down in his room with them…carries them out into the kitchen then back into his room." For Korin the reader, who transports them constantly with him, within himself, the problem indeed becomes that "there is only war and war everywhere, *even within himself*."[33]

In other words, as the reader of the manuscript to which he has just given the title *War and War* when he transferred it to the internet, as the carrier or mailman of the narrative called *War and War* that we are reading with and through him, Korin transposes irenicism to reading itself, to the act of reading that he embodies for us.

For the reader that he is for the readers that we are, getting out of this state of perpetual war that is coextensive with the text and its reading would, then, require transporting the four characters that he carries within himself toward an elsewhere, a place outside the text, an outside the text that would, à la Faust, be accessible only in or through the hypertext.

To be able to "put them down somewhere,"[34] as Korin says, to consign them and dismiss them, those four and the written text that constitutes them, would be equivalent to making reading into an interior exit, so to speak. It would be a sort of slit in the text, perhaps, this time not for an envelope containing another piece of writing to be inserted, but to provide an escape from within.

—∞

Korin repeatedly runs up against the impossibility of such an escape. He does not know what to do with the four characters: "They somehow stayed with him, were clinging to him, and he felt he couldn't get rid of them just like that, but what could he do, where and how could he solve the problem?"[35]

Korin seems seriously to want to *write something on the water*,"[36] to trace something out on the surface of the lake in Zurich at the edge of which he now stands. He draws the words "way out" "in the snow with his foot"[37] for the captain of the only vessel in sight, who thinks he is mad: "He thought he had misheard or misunderstood him, but no, just imagine, it seemed the guy really did want to do all that, to take a boat out and use it to write something on the water."[38] Korin's madness, however, is perfectly rigorous: logic dictates that only a form of writing that is not writing—one that would immediately be erased by liquification, like reading itself—could point to a way out of the text without immediately being caught back in the text, without becoming text in turn.

But it is winter, and there is no navigation on the lake. Korin will not be able to inscribe on the water the performative pointer toward the exit he so fervently seeks. At that point, the only alternative left for him is to take the four characters with him to the museum of contemporary art in Schaffhausen, where he knows — he had discovered this while looking at photographs when he was still in New York — that there is a peculiar sculpture that looks like a "a version of a prehistoric structure... something like an igloo,"[39] something that might shelter and contain, like a bubble, not only Korin the reader, but also those who live within him, those he cannot seem to deposit anywhere else than, perhaps, in this "remarkably light-looking, delicate contraption," in this "skeleton made of aluminum tubes filled in with broken, irregular panes of glass."[40]

It is thus there, in this igloo made of almost nothing, that is, we learn, the "world-famous sculpture by Mario Merz,"[41] one of the great artists of *Arte Povera* in Italy, it is in this sculpture that Korin would like to "spend an hour"[42] before ending things and in order to end them, in order to find the way out for himself and for the four he carries within himself. However, having been refused entry to the museum in the middle of the night, being therefore unable to reach Merz's igloo, all he can do is formulate one last request to the museum guard, who later will relay it to the director. The request is for a plaque to be put up, "a plaque screwed to the wall, with a single sentence engraved on it telling his story."[43]

Once he has in turn read, as we have, the manuscript entrusted to the provisional eternity of internet, the director agrees to the request:

> He turned on the computer, checked AltaVista... and saw with his own eyes that the manuscript really existed under the English title of War and War... what he had decided, he declared, is that there would be a plaque on the wall, a simple plaque, to tell the visitor what happened to György Korin in his last hours and it would say precisely what it said on the piece of paper, because the man deserved to find peace in the text of such a plaque, a man, the director lowered his voice, for whom the end was to be found in Schaffhausen.[44]

It is here, after the comma, that the narrative of *War and War* ends with a sort of hole or slit in the text, with a vast blank a few lines long, followed with an apparently redundant note:

> ...a man, the director lowered his voice, for whom the end was to be found in Schaffhausen,

> an end really to be found in Schaffhausen.[45]

Why the blank? And what does "really" (*tényleg*) mean here? It is not just a phrase for emphasis, as though the narrator wanted to drive the point home and insist that it really is over, that the narrative does indeed end. What "really" underlines here is not that the end truly took place, here under our very eyes, but rather that it took place there, outside, *in the real*. The indications given in the text after the last period should convince us of this.

Indeed, after finishing the narrative, we find first, on the inside of the back cover of the French edition, instructions for getting to Schaffhausen (by train, plane, or car). Since I could not go, I turned to the virtual ways of Google Street View, and as I arrived at the museum, which still today really does house Merz's igloo,[46] I can assure you that up to the left of the door as you exit the building, I saw the plaque that Korin requested, with the following text in German and in Hungarian: "This plaque marks the place where György Korin, the hero of the novel *War and War* by László Krasznahorkai, shot himself in the head. Search as he might, he could not find what he had called the Way Out."[47]

Isn't this plaque, which *really* exists,[48] paradoxically the way out that Korin seems to find precisely at the moment when he gives up on his search and has his failure engraved for eternity? And doesn't the blank, the few white lines in the narrative, figure this very exit,

on the edge of the text, dividing its end between an internal end
("the end was to be found in Schaffhausen") and an external end
("an end really to be found in Schaffhausen")?

Unless it is actually the other way around: unless Korin the
reader, being unable to find a way out for himself and for the characters he carries within *in* the text, ends up *forcing the text to exit
its own limits*, its boundaries, letting it spill over into reality. This
hypothesis seems to be confirmed by the existence of an internet
site that I ended up discovering (you can do the same) by typ-
ing, much as the Schaffhausen museum director did, the letters
"warandwar" in a search engine.

Among many results — reviews or commentaries on the novel of
one László Krasznahorkai — I stumble on a web page, www.warand-
war.com. Go see. You will read what I read, that is to say, the following notice: "Please be informed that this home page service has
been called off due to recurring overdue payment. Attempted mail
deliveries to Mr. G. Korin have been returned to sender with a note:
address unknown. Consequently, all data have been erased from
this home page."[49] I deduce that the manuscript bearing the title
War and War ended up being erased from the internet after Korin,
deceased, no longer made the necessary payments.

Beyond the fact that this very suppression seems to attest that
such a manuscript really did exist and that it was, in fact, transcribed onto the World Wide Web, there is something that even
the wariest, most incredulous reader cannot doubt, namely, that
the narrative published under the title *War and War* continues to
produce text beyond its apparent double end. It keeps expanding
and proliferating beyond the final period that should have put a
close to it. In short, it exceeds itself.

For there is, without contest, at least one extra sentence beyond
the novel, that is, the one on the plaque at the entrance to the
Schaffhausen museum. That is a sentence that was added to the
novel in reality. There are then several additional sentences on the
internet page we just read, signaling the erasure of the manuscript

of which Krasznahorkai's book nevertheless maintains many fragments and traces.

There are yet other sentences, always more sentences after what was supposed to be the end, for instance, on the site whose address is on the cover of the French edition, *Guerre et guerre* (https://guerreetguerre.wordpress.com), near the slit that is just waiting for us to insert the envelope from "Isaiah Has Come," like the good mailmen or couriers that we are. On this site, we find, among other things, the story of Mario Merz's visit to the Schaffhausen museum (where he apparently was furious with the director who had not let Korin in), then his visit to Gyula (Korin's hometown, and also, as it happens, hometown to Krasznahorkai) to consider building an igloo, a project interrupted by the artist's death. There are also photographs of the plaque and of its inauguration in Schaffhausen, in the presence, by the way, of one László Krasznahorkai, who stands solemnly next to the museum guard.

In other words, the text of *War and War*—but which text? the manuscript Korin found, that we read with him, reading him read? that of the novel that tells the story of this reading? that of the sites that prolong it?—is not watertight. It oozes; it leaks. Like the Faustian hyperbook Valéry described, it is a text that keeps on being written, constantly overflowing its limits, chipping away at what is supposed to be outside the text. Even more than the hypertext Faust signed, Korin's text tends toward being ever less distinguishable from the general text that we would like to call "reality."

Isn't that also what the perpetual war of the title, *War and War*, signifies? For if Korin did not find the way out (peace), if the war (and war and war, with no opposite), whose battlefield was now "within himself" continues thus beyond the end, moving over the blank and pouring into a text without borders, into the general sentence of the internet, then is it not the case that I am, you are, we readers are, like Korin our *prolocutor* or prophet, looking for a way out?

Among the possible ways out that the text of *War and War* produces in the same movement that immediately closes them again (reinscribing them in this very text from which they should provide escape), there was, as we saw, the igloo, described in the English translation as a "remarkably light-looking, delicate contraption." "Delicate" is the translation of the Hungarian *leheletfinom*, a word that more literally signifies the flimsiness of a breath (*lehelet*). The English translator has glossed the adjective with a phrase, "a bubble of air," that gives perhaps too much consistency to the almost nothing of the refuge where Korin the reader thinks he may be able to get out of the text in the text.[50]

The extreme narrowness of the way out for which Korin hopes is as thin as a breath; such is the only exit for the one who reads, the one who wants to *leave the text precisely by sticking to it*. It is to be found at the text's surface, in the ungraspable lightness of a fold that should not be considered to have any density at all, not even that of a bubble, for that would congeal it into a textual consistency, therewith sealing up the tiny crack that stood ajar.

It is tempting to see Korin's infraslim igloo as an irenicist allegory for reading's proper place, the place without a place that Blanchot considered the realm of "the lightness, the irresponsibility, and the innocence" of the reader.[51] Yet the Hungarian term *leheletfinom* indicates not only an absence of thickness in which the protagonist, reading with and for us, would like to be able to be in peace. Beyond hyperbolic slimness, what resonates in this word is precisely the breath (*lehelet*), the breathing that might well be that of the reader, Korin's or our own. Is it not then there, in the diaphanous breath, that reading could exit from the text, that it could detach from the text in the very same movement by which it dives in?

No more and probably less than Korin, who represents us, do we have a way out other than one that has the slight (in)consistency of a breath. Like him, and probably even more than he, we are condemned to make our way back and forth through the infinite text that he ended up making *War and War* into, a hypertext whose limits cannot be reached because it spreads throughout reality. Our impossible way out of this general sentence (whether we call it the internet or world literature) could, then, only be *a way out of the sentence in the sentence.* And it is that escape, one no sooner ajar than closed again, that, borrowing from Hobbes's prophetic typology one last time, I would call *pre-diction.*

Why that word?

To hear it properly, we must first understand what phrasing means, understand the power of the sentence that, as he explains to the translator's lover in New York, Korin experiences for a few pages before realizing that what is at stake in the manuscript he holds is "the way out." Let us listen to Korin speaking about the phrasal texture of what he is reading and thus of what we are reading through him, over his narratological shoulder, so to speak:[52]

> There is an order in the sentences: words, punctuation, periods, commas all in place, said Korin, and yet ... the sentences seemed to have lost their reason, not just growing ever longer and longer but galloping desperately onward in a harum-scarum scramble ... once a sentence begins it doesn't want to stop ... the words begin to fill the sentences, leaping over each other, piling up ... dense, concentrated, enclosed, a suffocating airless throng of pieces, that's how they are, that's right, Korin nodded, it was as if — *all the sentences* — each sentence was of vital importance, a matter of *life and death*, the whole developing and moving at a dizzy rate.[53]

This moment of maximal textual density (it is reminiscent of the elocutionary crases in "Isaiah Has Come"), this moment at which the sentences in the manuscript seem to want to coagulate in their effort to contain everything, as if they were freezing in their very speed, this moment is also the one at which Korin, who usually works from memory, knowing the text by heart at this point, suddenly for once needs actually to see the manuscript: "He got up, left the room, then returned a moment later with a big wad of paper, sat down beside the woman, picked up the manuscript and searched through it for a while, then, begging her pardon for just this once having to have the text in front of him, chose a few pages."[54] As the text becomes denser, Korin's reading becomes more intense, more attentive.

Strangely, however, this moment of intense concentration on the text actually leads Korin to detach from it. For at the very moment when Korin thinks he has identified the key to the mystery of the manuscript—he "understood everything"[55]—at the very moment, then, when his reading and ours with it has "time to mature to a point at which it could at last become clear,"[56] in short, when he realizes that the whole story converges toward the search for a way out, Korin the reader flips into a reading regime that is somewhat like Lust's in *"My Faust."* He suddenly becomes almost indifferent, taking notes and reading mechanically, distractedly: "He read the enormous, ever longer sentences and typed them into the computer though his mind wasn't on it but somewhere else altogether, he told the woman, so everything that remained of the last chapter of the manuscript practically typed itself."[57] It seems that Korin's reading strays further from the text in the very same movement by which it adheres most stringently to the text and captures it for understanding.

Just as the monster sentence or the world sentence goes mad— "a single monstrous, infernal, all-absorbing sentence"[58]—just as it oscillates wildly between the speed of light and infinite length, the reading is also pulled between two extremes: maximum focus on the text (for once, Korin needs to have it in front of his eyes) and complete detachment from it.

What happens there, in this *dis-contraction*[59] of reading that echoes the systoles and diastoles of the text's phrasing, is something like what Hobbes admits at the end of *Leviathan*, although it went against the grain for him (namely, that "it is natural for men, at one and the same time, both to proceed in reading, and to lose their attention").[60] Or like what de Certeau described as "absolute reading," reading that is just about to disconnect (*absolvere*) from the written at the point where it touches it tangentially.

Let us try, once more, to get closer to the anagnosological tangent point, to the strange and paradoxical movement of reading that goes beyond the text, takes off from it, precisely by adhering to it, by sticking closely to its development as though the better to get ahead of it. To understand what is at stake here, let us follow the course, or the racing, of another of Krasznahorkai's short narratives, "On Velocity," which describes an apparently much larger — crazier — attempt at overtaking than that of the reading of a few lines or pages since the narrator wants "to leave the Earth behind."[61]

I refer to that story here in order to clarify what I would like to call the *pre-diction* as a *way out of the sentence in the sentence* because the story seems to want to give the key to its own allegorical reading by asserting, at some point in one of its meanders, that "*the Earth is thought*."[62] If such is the case, however, if the word "Earth" can or must be replaced by the word "thought," and it is then thought that must be overtaken in the course of the infinite sentence that describes and mimes the narrator's racing over the surface of the Earth, then what strange reading movement carries us, the readers, away?

Let us see:

> I want to leave the Earth behind, so I dash past the bridge over the stream by the meadow, past the reindeer-feeding trough in the dark of the forest, turning at Monowitz at the corner of Schuhkammer and Kleiderkammer, into the street, in my desire to move faster than the Earth in whatever direction this thought has taken me, for everything has converged to such a point of departure, leaving everything behind, leaving behind the Earth, and I set off, rushing instinctively, doing the right thing by rushing, because ... I am heading ... West, which is right, if only because the Earth spins from left to right, that is to say from a Western to an Eastern direction, that is right, that's how things are, that's how it felt right, was right, from the first half-fraction of the instant [*pillanat*] in which I started, since everything moves

most definitely from West to East: the building, the morning kitchen, the table with its cup, the cup with its steaming emerald-colored tea and the scent spiraling upward, and all the blades of grass in the meadow that are pearled with morning dew, and the empty reindeer-feeder in the dark of the forest, all of these — each and every one — moves according to its nature from West to East.[63]

The Earth, as we know, does turn on its own axis from left to right, just as a text is read left to right. The world enunciated by the infinite sentence and the very saying of this world sentence describe a movement that goes in the same direction. And at first, it is *against* this rotation or this progressing that "I" sets out, as though it were a matter of running or phrasing against the prevailing movement, from right to left.

Very quickly, however — in a moment that lasts only the fraction of an instant, the batting of an eye (*pillanat*, says the Hungarian, like the German *Augenblick*) — "I" turns around:

Or rather, no, as I painfully realized in the second half of the instant [*pillanat*], no alas, of course not in that direction, opposing its movement being precisely the worst choice, my instincts had led me to turn in precisely the wrong direction at the corner, over the field, and past the dark of the forest, when I should have chosen to move in the same direction, from West to East as Earth did...and so, in the blink of an eye [*egy szemrebbenés alatt*], I immediately turned around on my axis.[64]

It is after this reversal that we find the allegorical key that encouraged us to read this race as an attempt to get ahead of thought in the course of the sentence. And we meet this equivalence between Earth and thought at exactly the moment at which it becomes a matter of respiration — of breathing, of breath — and a certain *betweenness* to which we will return:

From West to East, according with the movement of the Earth, since it is precisely in this fashion, in precisely this manner, of course, I'd have to run in order to be faster than the Earth, running with it so to speak, from a western direction to an eastern direction, and ... I was already faster, since my velocity now comprehended that of the Earth, that is to say it included it without my having to do much more than move a muscle, and this way, by running over the Earth's surface from West to East, I had made the task so much simpler, I could breathe ever more easily [*lélegeztem egyre boldogabban*], since the air was fresh out here [*idekint*], I was enjoying the night or the dawn of freedom, or something between the two [*a kettő között*], I was locked into that interval between night and dawn, feeling perfectly calm, because thinking that I now chose the correct direction, I was moving faster than the Earth, since *the Earth is thought*, as I thought right at the beginning, and now I wanted to move faster than thought, to leave it behind [*lehagyni a gondolatot*].[65]

What is thought if not a sentence, a saying, be it silent, in which words that have not yet been pronounced run into each other or collide, as happens in Korin's diction or in the manuscript he transcribes? And who (or what) is attempting here to get ahead of this thought? Who is this "I" who would like to outstrip it? It is perhaps, in the end, nothing other than the very movement of the world sentence in its course or racing (remember that in *War and War* the "sentences" of the manuscript start "galloping desperately onward").

For we, readers, who follow the sentence and lend it our breath as well as our voice, for we who run with it until we are out of breath, it is as though we were experiencing a phrasing trying to get ahead of the phrase, a saying rushing ahead of the said that nevertheless carries it. That would be the most rigorous description of what de Certeau called "absolute reading," a reading that breaks away from the sentence, even as it ties into it most closely.

The phrasing detaching from the sentence for a moment, the saying rushing ahead of the said: this dehiscence is precisely what we should call *pre-diction*: when reading, in this literally pro-phetic moment, reaches ahead of what it reads, when it becomes a precursor (*avant-courier*).

Praedictor, said Hobbes, when speaking of prophets. Even before they predict this or that (before they convey this or that fore-told content), however, the pre-diction at stake here is about speed, or rather the speed difference in reading diction. Pre-diction is the name for the speed differential between the reader's phrasing and the sentence of the text, the former overtaking the latter, shooting toward the text's future like an elastic band stretched to breaking point that yet still, barely, holds together.

The gap or distance that reading thus opens is only as thick as a breath: *leheletfinom*, as *War and War*'s narrator says of the bubble structure of the igloo (but he used the same adjective about the sentences of the manuscript he found in the archives).[66] The infinitesimal, the infraslim margin by which the reader is ahead of what he is reading, opens an interstice between the text and reader that is as fragile as writing on water.

And the breathing that reading gives to the text by hollowing out an air bubble in it, that breath is happy, insists the narrator of "On Velocity:" "I could breathe ever more easily [*lélegeztem egyre boldogabban*: ever more happily], since the air was fresh out here [*idekint*], I was enjoying the night or the dawn of freedom, or something between the two [*a kettő között*], I was locked into [*bezárva*] that interval between night and dawn, feeling perfectly calm [*egészen megnyugodtam*]."[67] It feels good, in this betweenness, in this interval in which the one who says "I" (whoever: me, you, any reader, or any move toward reading) is enclosed. It seems that what one meets there is calm: something like a fleeting, intermittent easing of tensions that has some distant relation to the absolute peace Korin so desired.

How, though, can one be a prisoner in the outdoors, where things breathe, where things are fresh? It is as if, paradoxically, the text's "I" were cloistered in open space. For the outside in question here — the exit to peace, to ending the war and war and war of the text and its reading — that outside lasts for only the blink of an eye; it opens only long enough to catch, or hold, one's breath. This way out, this passage, has just the consistency of a systole-diastole, of what I called a *dis-contraction*: reading's phrasing pulses in this rhythmical opening, taking off from the text with the same momentum that allows it to stick to the text's progress.

Archereading

Are you still there? A little like Kierkegaard at the end of his *Stages on Life's Way*, I am afraid that I may have been left behind alone as you perhaps took off on a tangent. If you can still hear me, I suggest we catch our breath together, dear reader, after the mad dash that has led us here.

I'm a little dazed, as you probably are. I am starting to wonder how we are going to get out of here, what sort of way out we can invent together. Should I launch into a *Leviathan*-like summary, for instance, doing accounts the way Hobbes does? I can just imagine this final accounting: whereas Jean Paul ends *Titan*,[1] his novel, with an anagnosological jubilee that offers to erase all the reader's debts, here, the final tally would force you to do a complex calculation in order to establish and verify the sum for everything that has been accumulated up to now. You would have to go over each one of the debits and credits in order for us to settle our accounts before going our separate ways, you and me.

This long concluding sum might, in sum, look like this:

✓ In the first chapter after the Introduction, by listening to Hoffmann's "The Sandman," I suggested that the reading voice, when it is not repressed in order to let the read text transpire, brings out the intimate uncanniness of reading.

✓ In the second chapter, a brief historical investigation led me to show that the reading scene is actually occupied not by one, but by several voices (one belonging to the text, another to the phonographic anagnost, another to the imperative . . .), that form at least a triangle, probably a square.

✓ In the third and fourth chapters, I invoked two great reading moments in Plato to observe how the vocal roles also become positions of power (the *erastēs* and the *erōmenos*, the slave) and how these positions can be permuted or reversed, notably by rereading.

✓ In the fifth chapter, moving through *Philosophy in the Bedroom* with Lacan, I strove to auscultate the categorical imperative of reading that threads through the text while remaining confined in an untouchable outside.

✓ After a brief sixth chapter in the form of an intermission in a courtroom (the vocal reading scene appeared more than ever like a force field), in the seventh chapter we read Italo Calvino very closely, not only in order to look into the gendered traits of he or she (that is the question) whom we agreed to call the *readee*, but also and above all to experience the speed differential that operates at the heart of reading and detaches it from the text by drawing it ahead of the text.

✓ In the eighth chapter (are you still with me? can you still keep count?), we stopped to take stock of two opposite, but connected, conceptions of reading, oscillating between binding (when reading is gathering) and unbinding (when it tends to become absolute, infinitive).

✓ In the ninth chapter we laid out the political consequences of binding or unbinding reading by following, step by step, the parallel construction of the state and of the reader in the reading machine that is Hobbes's *Leviathan*.

✓ In the tenth chapter, we took stock of the extraordinary acceleration of reading in the era of world literature and hypertext before trying to avert a Faustian wreck and save a certain desire for a reading that might be conjugated in the subjunctive.

✓ Finally, in the eleventh chapter, we followed the racing of the reader through László Krasznahorkai's *War and War* until the speed differential that builds up in it opens the ephemeral and infraslim gap, the bubble in which we find... what exactly?

Where does this laborious accounting lead us as we make our way through it and are close to exhaustion ("Dear solitary, tired... reader")? Does this taxing reckoning lead us toward the moment of jubilation we have been hoping for, the moment that Hobbes announced with these words: "As to the whole doctrine, I see not yet, but the principles of it are true and proper; and the ratiocination solid?"[2] Or is it the case that instead of leading us toward the triumphant and irritating tautology that any conclusion is bound to be (I hate conclusions), the accumulation only underlines a hiatus, a lacuna, a fault line that calls for correction?

We have encountered several times, leaving it somewhat up in the air, a phrase that Benjamin borrowed from Hofmannsthal. It is still waiting for the attention it deserves. Before we turn out the light, like Calvino's two readers, let us come back to that phrase, the better to measure what might be held in that bubble of breath that reading creates between the phrasing and the sentence.

"Read what was never written": this formula, borrowed from Hofmannsthal's lyrical drama, *Death and the Fool*, appears twice in Benjamin's writings. The first occurrence is in 1933, in a brief essay titled "On the Mimetic Faculty," the second in 1940, in the paralipomena and variants of *On the Concept of History* (both texts were published posthumously).

In Hofmannsthal's play, it is Death itself who nods and says of men: "How wonderful these humans are, indeed, / Who do explain [*deuten*] the inexplicable, / And what was never writ, they read [*lesen*]."[3] When Benjamin picks up on these words in 1940, he does so in a context in which reading is, for him, too, synonymous with interpretation:

If one looks upon history as a text, then one can say of it what a recent author has said of literary texts — namely, that the past has left in them images comparable to those registered by a light-sensitive plate: "The future alone possesses developers strong enough to reveal the image in all its details. Many pages in Marivaux or Rousseau contain a mysterious meaning which the first readers of those texts could not fully have deciphered."... The historical method is a philological method based on the book of life. "Read what was never written," runs a line in Hofmannsthal. The reader one should think of here is the true historian.[4]

In this context, everything indicates that Hofmannsthal's verse, introduced as it is by the reference to a "recent author," should not be taken literally: "Read what was never written" here means *reading what has never yet been decoded*, what remains to be unveiled. It is, then, a matter of reading what is already written in a writing that, granted, is still awaiting revelation (like a photographic film), but that is in fact already inscribed, engraved somewhere.

When it first occurs in Benjamin's writings, in 1933, Hofmannsthal's verse seems instead to mean something else altogether. It stands in quotation marks, without any mention of the source, at the beginning of the last paragraph of the text: "'To read what was never written.' Such reading [*dies Lesen*] is the most ancient: reading prior to all languages [*das Lesen vor aller Sprache*], from entrails, the stars, or dances. Later the mediating link of a new kind of reading [*ein neues Lesens*], of runes and hieroglyphs, came into use."[5] Here, it is thus a matter of a reading that not only precedes this or that historically attested type of writing (the runic alphabet or hieroglyphs), but that goes even further back than any constituted language whose inscription might be deciphered. We might call this radically antescriptural and prelinguistic reading *archereading*.[6]

This reading that goes back to a past immemorial, in the times before texts, also moves toward what comes from beyond the text, from the future. Benjamin's prophesizing archereading prefigures the reading detached from writing about which de Certeau wrote so compellingly, that is, the tangential reading that overtakes the text and takes off from it. Indeed, it is remarkable to note that in his "Doctrine of the Similar," a brief essay written a few months before "On the Mimetic Faculty," of which it is a sort of anticipated variant, Benjamin considers "that reading from stars, entrails, and coincidences" (*dieses Herauslesen aus Sternen, Eingeweiden, Zufällen*) as a sort of "absolute reading" (as I propose to translate what he calls "*das Lesen schlechthin*" there—in other words, reading pure and simple, "reading per se," reading par excellence).[7]

Reading in this way, reading absolutely, reading *beyond the text*, comes down to dreaming of sovereign autonomy for reading, an unconditional freedom that would free reading from any obligation to repeat what is written. Reading would be sheer path breaking, pure invention. A reading that could be called *purely prophetic*, drawn forward by a movement of anticipation that did not announce any encrypted content that was to become decipherable one day or anything that was in some way already inscribed and waiting to be said again: just *a pure reading to come.*

Exempting itself from any submission to a textual instance, such a reading would, of course, no longer be a reading worthy of the name. It would be an aporetic or impossible reading, one that reading, in the strict sense, must always measure itself against in order to invent itself each time in a singular manner *as it moves through the text.*

In his "Doctrine of the Similar," Benjamin describes absolute reading as "magical" (it is the reading of the "astrologer [who] reads the future in the stars"), to distinguish it from "profane" reading, reading in its usual meaning (the way "the schoolboy reads his ABC book"). And he seems to be surprised by what he calls the "peculiar ambiguity [*dem merkwürdigen Doppelsinn*] of the word 'reading.'"[8]

Yet pushing Benjamin's surprise perhaps a little further than what he himself would have recognized, shouldn't we suppose that this double meaning of the term is in a certain way the very meaning of reading, its proper sense? In other words, might we not think that reading, as such, is always torn, pulled to a breaking point between the mechanical repetition of an anagnost and the address to a readee to come?

—☙

As we have seen, this tension always plays out in a speed differential between the voices or the vocal instances that inhabit the reading scene, whether that scene takes place tacitly within us or noisily in front of us. It is a difference between fluidities and resistances that operate at the heart of the anagnosological output. And in order to hear it, one must give up the all too common idea that there might be an adequate rhythm of reading, as one of Blaise Pascal's *Pensées* suggests ("when we read too fast or too slow, we understand nothing").[9] This same idea can be found in the conclusion of Benjamin's "Doctrine of the Similar." There, he does insist on the importance of "swiftness in reading" (*Schnelligkeit im Lesen*), but his concern is to obtain "the necessary tempo" (*einem notwendigen Tempo*), that is to say an imposed cadence, one that is congruent.[10]

If, then, we lend an ear and give up on finding a proper or conforming pace, we start to hear the friction of diverging anagnosological speeds of which we have encountered so many examples.

✓ There are, of course, all the prophets who, in Hobbes or Krasznahorkai, embody the tangential nature of a reading that is projected toward the absolute while being held back in the text.

✓ There is also, if one thinks about it, Phaedrus reading the beginning of Lysias's speech over and over again for Socrates, as though the *erōmenos* who wanted to prolong his *erastēs'* speech by keeping going were condemned by the readee's imperative to treading water: "Stop" (*pausai*), says Socrates, before ordering him to read on.[11]

✓ I could show you many other moments in which, as in Sade's ellipses, reading is both anchored in the text (sewn to it) and carried elliptically beyond it (reading skims the text, whether out of disgust or excitement).

✓ Most especially in Calvino, we were able to observe how different speeds cross the reading scene, with the different roles that structure it. Thus, at the beginning of chapter four of *If on a Winter's Night . . .* , Calvino notes that "when someone else is reading," that is to say, when we readees listen to an anagnost reading, "it is difficult to make your attention coincide with the tempo of his reading: the voice goes either too fast or too slow."[12]

✓ Calvino even went a step further in dislocating the anagnosological field since he introduced a speed differential in the very readee, who was split into two instances, one of which "is always at least one step ahead" of the other.[13]

I realize that I have started ✓ counting, ✓ adding, ✓ summing again. Forgive me. It is irresistible, as irresistible as all efforts to reduce the speed differential to a constant, measured, and checked progression, like the one presupposed not only by Hobbes's Leviathanesque reading machine, but also by the friendly feature on my e-reader that warns me how many minutes reading I have left in a given chapter or warns me that I have reached the predefined time allotted to daily reading.

Far be it from me, however, to suggest that reading becoming hypertextual or connected, reading becoming networked, is only about the production of quantifications such as the one that so irked me ("4 other people have highlighted this section"). The new media also become pretexts for reading scenes in which the polyphony of voices is reinvented in new forms. If you explore the world of BookTubers (influencers who post videos about books on YouTube), you will find novel anagnosological situations that oscillate between festivities that celebrate an idealized synchronization of voices (for instance, "reading marathons," *readathons*, during which all the participants try to read a certain number of pages in a given time), on the one hand, and, on the other hand, virtual spaces that accommodate the most extreme disconnection (silent-reading clubs that have recently flourished on the internet since the coronavirus pandemic, each person reading for themselves, deep in their own book, but connected to others doing the same).

Some of the most remarkable clips (for instance, those posted by jessethereader, who has more than four hundred thousand followers on YouTube) are really small treatises on readers' faces and expressions as they read (imagine if Socrates had filmed Phaedrus reading Lysias!), whereas others compile the thoughts that cross the mind of a reader while reading (what would happen if Lust shared her distracted ideas with thousands of followers?).

The most daring futurists, such as Cyrano de Bergerac predicting future audiobooks, would never have imagined some of the reading scenes that flourish nowadays.[14] I am convinced, however, that the triangulated or quadrangulated structure whose story we have traced, from Plato to Valéry's hyper-Faust and beyond, provides the basis on which they can and must be analyzed. Who reads for whom? Which anagnost(s) for which readee(s)? Who orders, or suggests, or orchestrates, the reading, according to which imperatives?

If you find it surprising or irritating to hear me thus compare anagnosological situations that are as distant from one another in time as one of Plato's dialogues from a BookTube video, give me at least one more moment for a brief retrospective look at how reading media have evolved.

The book, as we know it, did not exist in such a form in Plato's time. What we hold in our hands is the modern version of what the Roman Empire invented under the name of *codex*, that is to say, a book with pages made from parchment, an animal-sourced material. As of the second century AD, such paginated books gradually replaced the old *volumen* ("rolled up" in Latin), the papyrus roll on which text was written in columns and that had to be unrolled with one hand while it was rolled up with the other.

Agamben discerns two different relations to time in these bibliographic media: he suggests that the *codex* reflected "the linear conception of time specific of the Christian world," whereas the rolled-up *volumen* "conformed better to the cyclical conception of time typical of Antiquity."[15] He goes on to suggest that these formats both survive in the computer screen, which, "like the book...enables pagination" while allowing vertical browsing "like in a roll, from top to bottom."[16]

Well! Isn't that exactly what happens in the triangulated or quadrangulated reading scenes we exhumed from antiquity or in the Sadian shadows of the Enlightenment? Just as the screen is the place where the *volumen*'s ghost comes to haunt the *codex* pagination, the characters of the anagnost and the readee come to inhabit the ebooks and reading clubs in which web users congregate today.

⁓᧓

Dear reader, it is time for us to part. Rather than subject you to an awkward leave-taking scene, I suggest that instead we read one together. Let us open a few pages — the last ones to which we will listen side by side. The title is "Unpacking My Library; A Talk about Book Collecting."

In 1931, Walter Benjamin, him again, recounts a scene we have all lived through: opening boxes full of books that are piled up and await, as the boxes are opened, decisions about how to file them and distribute them on the bookshelves of their new habitat.

Why read these pages today? And how are they a farewell? To what?

"Not yet [*noch nicht*]": in the "disorder of crates that have been wrenched open," among "piles of volumes that are seeing daylight again after two years of darkness," these two words punctuate the first sentences of the story (the books are "not yet on the shelves," they are "not yet touched by the mild boredom of order")[17] as though to put off the moment at which the move, the transfer, will be stabilized into a catalogue. For what interests Benjamin is not the accumulation once it has been petrified, but rather the very movement of collecting (he offers insight "into collecting rather than a collection.")[18]

And yet, despite the delightful details and the touching anecdotes Benjamin offers about his own practice, despite the memories of auctions or memorable acquisitions he shares, the person of the collector and his art increasingly give way to the volumes themselves.

The "not yet" that punctuated the beginning of the narrative becomes an "already" ("it is way past midnight [already]")[19] that marks a double disappearance: the historical disappearance of the figure of the bibliophile or bibliomaniac ("time is running out for the type that I am discussing here,"[20] writes Benjamin melancholically) and the fictional or autobiographical (probably both) disappearance of the narrator of "Unpacking My Library," the story we are reading, who in the end disappears into the collection he has just unpacked (the piece ends with: "Now he is going to disappear inside, as is only fitting").[21]

What happened in the meantime, in the time between "not yet" and "already"?

In German, collecting is *sammeln*, with its resonance of the *Sammlung*, the collectedness or gathering to which Heidegger was so attached. In French and in English, with their Latin origins, the names for collectors and collections and the term for reader (*lecteur*) share the memory of the Latin *lectio* as a harvesting.

Yet in Benjamin, the collector is an extremely paradoxical reader figure. Indeed, "Unpacking My Library" is above all a tribute to the *nonuse* of books, to the relation to books that leaves aside "their usefulness" and considers only the "the scene, the stage, of their fate."[22] What counts is not the value the books have *for us*, whether use or exchange value. A real bibliophile does not think of selling a book he has acquired or really of reading it.

Benjamin goes so far as to assert that "the nonreading of books" is "characteristic of collectors."[23] Of course, this does not mean that collectors never read, but rather that when they do, they do not have a collector's relationship to the books they read. That is why Benjamin uses the past tense to refer to what he calls the "militant age" of his library, a bygone era "when no book was allowed to enter it without its certification, without having been read."[24]

The point is that the library, as a pure collection, begins only when both forced-march reading and book commerce end. It starts when books reach a *fate that is theirs, without us,* where the collector can buy a book "to give it its freedom."[25]

What happens, then, at midnight, when the collector disappears both from the historical scene and from the scene of the narrative we are reading? What happens when he is on the brink of literally being absorbed by his library in the last lines of the text? When he rushes into the library and evaporates?

From the perspective we have shared, dear reader, this scene of nocturnal farewells is one of the extremes toward which reading tends, when the reader fades, as is only fitting, when he slips away, allows himself to be forgotten. ("The book," Blanchot explains, "needs the reader . . . to declare itself a thing without an author and hence without a reader."[26])For it is at this point that books awaken and start living their lives (who knows, maybe they even speak to each other?).[27] This is the point when reading tends toward becoming a pure infinitive, a pure anagnosological event without a reading subject.

In 1933, in "On the Mimetic Faculty" and "Doctrine of the Similar," Benjamin gestures toward an archereading without a text. Two years earlier, in "Unpacking My Library," was he entertaining the idea of an archereading without a reader?

We would have to see. We would have to auscultate carefully certain phrases in which the collector, even as he embodies the disappearing reader, persists in the narrative and insists on asserting his presence and even his future.[28] But midnight has struck; there is no time left. What we can be sure of is that by pulling reading toward these two extremes, the disappearance of the text and the disappearance of the reader, Benjamin goes even further than de

Certeau and his politics of absolute reading in seeming to dream of a total unbinding at the heart of the reading scene.

Consequently, the diverging adverbs — "not yet," "already" — that punctuate the narrative of Benjamin's library (it seems to be the reverse of Faust's library, in which the Student perceives the accumulation, "inch by inch, century by century, [of] a monument of the UNREADABLE"),[29] these temporal markers, which point in opposite directions, should be heard as signaling toward a speed differential pushed to the extreme: in the (non)reading scene of "Unpacking My Library," the absolute speed that could skim over the text without touching it, seems to coincide with the absolute slowness that would remain at the threshold of the text without entering.

I am dreaming. I see the infinitive of pure reading (without a subject) and the subjunctive of the pure desire to read (without a text) coming together. And I think of that rainy reading that one of Calvino's characters talks about, of the "it is reading" that sounds like an "it is raining." And I also think of Lust and think how much I would have liked her to still be reading [*qu'elle lût encore*]. As for you, you are about to finish *Powers of Reading*, aren't you? Are you? Are you still reading? Are you no longer reading?

Notes

PREFACE TO THE ENGLISH-LANGUAGE EDITION

1. See Emmanuel Macron's speech, June 17, 2021, in Château-Thierry, elysee.fr/emmanuel-macron/2021/06/17/la-lecture-grande-cause-nationale-se-mobiliser-pour-la-langue-francaise. See also Joe Biden's proclamation, March 1, 2022, whitehouse.gov/briefing-room/presidential-actions/2022/03/01/a-proclamation-on-read-across-america-day-2022.

2. George Ticknor, *Life of William Hickling Prescott* (London: Routledge, 1864), p. 87. To be precise, there are a few, rare occurrences in French of the term *lectaire* (readee) in the sense of the act of reading's addressee. The term thus appears—perhaps for the first time—in Catherine J. Spenser's remarkable study of Michel Deville's film, *La lectrice* (The reader). In a note, she specifies that "in order to avoid endless and boring circumlocutions ('the one to whom she reads...') I took the liberty of this neologism, along the same lines as 'narratee.'" "*La lectrice:* Six personnages en quête de texte," *French Review* 67.2 (1993), pp. 301 and 312.

3. See Peter Szendy, *Listen: A History of Our Ears*, trans. Charlotte Mandell (New York: Fordham University Press, 2008), pp. 1–3 and 11, and *Of Stigmatology: Punctuation as Experience*, trans. Jan Plug (New York: Fordham University Press, 2018), p. 42. I proposed and developed the idea of the listenee in "How Many Ears? or, The Place of the Listenee," *alienocene*, November 26, 2022, https://alienocene.com/2022/11/26/how-many-ears-or-the-place-of-the-listenee.

4. François Rabelais, *Gargantua and Pantagruel*, trans. M. A. Screech (London: Penguin Books, 2006), p. 643.

5. See William Nelson, "From 'Listen, Lordings' to 'Dear Reader,'" *University of Toronto Quarterly* 46.2 (1976–1977), p. 114.

6. Araceli Tinajero, *El Lector: A History of the Cigar Factory Reader*, trans. Judith E. Grasberg (Austin: University of Texas Press, 2010), pp. xiii–xiv.

7. Quoted in Tinajero, *El Lector*, p. 20.

8. *Morning Tribune* (Tampa), December 22, 1903, p. 2.

9. Ibid.

10. Wen Gálvez, *Tampa: Impresiones de emigrado* (Tampa: Establecimento tipografico Cuba, 1897), pp. 178–79, author's translation.

11. Michel de Certeau, who advocated for the advent of "an autonomy of the practice of reading underneath scriptural imperialism," writes: "A politics of reading must thus be articulated on an analysis that, describing practices that have long been in effect, makes them politicizable." "Reading as Poaching," in *The Practice of Everyday Life*, trans. Stephen Rendall (Berkeley: University of California Press, 1984), pp. 169 and 173.

12. *El Diario de Tampa*, September 25, 1908, p. 2.

13. Fabio Morábito, *Home Reading Service: A Novel*, trans. Curtis Bauer (New York: Other Press, 2021), p. 33. Warm thanks to Laurent Evrard, bookseller at the wonderful bookshop Le Livre in Tours, France, for having recommended this.

14. Alexandra Alter and Elizabeth A. Harris, "Spotify Makes a Bet on Audiobooks," *New York Times*, September 20, 2022, https://www.nytimes.com/2022/09/20/books/spotify -audiobooks.html.

15. See Matthew Rubery, *The Untold Story of the Talking Book* (Cambridge, MA: Harvard University Press, 2016).

16. Octave Uzanne, "The End of Books," *Scribner's Magazine* 16.2, August 1894, pp. 227–28.

17. Edward Bellamy, "With the Eyes Shut," *Harper's New Monthly Magazine*, October 1889, p. 738.

18. Ibid.

19. Elizabeth Gaskell, Letter 273, in J. A. V. Chapple and Arthur Pollard, eds., *The Letters of Mrs. Gaskell* (Manchester, UK: Manchester University Press, 1966), p. 373.

...HAVE YOU STARTED READING?

1. It would no doubt be more precise to say with Michel Foucault that "what the apparatuses and institutions operate is, in a sense, a micro-physics of power, whose field

of validity is situated in a sense between these great functionings and the bodies them-selves with their materiality and forces." *Discipline and Punish: The Birth of the Prison*, trans. Alan Sheridan (New York: Vintage Books, 1955), p. 26. One could also consider reading as the field of a "micropolitics" in the sense in which Gilles Deleuze and Félix Guattari understood the term when they said that "every politics is simultaneously a *macropoltics* and a *micropolitics*." *A Thousand Plateaus: Capitalism and Schizophrenia*, trans. Brian Massumi (Minneapolis: University of Minnesota Press, 1987), p. 213.

2. On subvocalization, see, for example, Alexander Pollatsek, "The Role of Sound in Silent Reading," in *The Oxford Handbook of Reading*, eds. Alexander Pollatsek and Rebecca Treiman (Oxford: Oxford University Press, 2015), pp. 197–201. Five eminent scientists — Keith Rayner, Elizabeth Scotter, Michael Masson, Mary Potter, and Rebecca Treiman — recently returned to this thorny issue. They write: "Another claim that underlies speed-reading courses is that, through training, speed readers can increase reading efficiency by inhibiting subvocalization. This is the speech that we often hear in our heads when we read. This inner speech is an abbreviated form of speech that is not heard by others and that may not involve overt movements of the mouth but that is, nevertheless, experienced by the reader. Speed-reading proponents claim that this inner voice is a habit that carries over from fact that we learn to read out loud before we start reading silently and that inner speech is a drag on reading speed.... However, research on normal reading challenges this claim.... Attempts to eliminate inner speech have been shown to result in impairments in comprehension. "So Much to Read, So Little Time," *Psychological Science in the Public Interest* 17.1 (January 2016), p. 23.

3. For an overview of Ulises Carrión's work, see the beautiful catalogue of the exhibition organized at the Reina Sofía Museum in Madrid, Guy Schraenen, ed., *Ulises Carrión: Dear reader. Don't read* (Madrid: Departamento de Actividades Editoriales del Museo Nacional Centro de Arte Reina Sofía, 2016). A reproduction of this double con-straint, as dizzying as it is simple ("you who are already reading, don't read!") is on pp. 112–13. (Thanks to Nora Edén for bringing this work to my attention.) As Jean-Luc Nancy also says, "A book is an address or an appeal. Beneath the melodic line of its singing there intones, without interruption, the continuous bass of its invitation, of its request, injunction, or prayer: 'Read me! Read me!' (And that prayer murmurs still, even when the author declares 'Don't read me!' or 'Throw my book away!')" *On the Commerce of Thinking: Of Books and Bookstores*, trans. David Wills (New York: Fordham University Press, 2019), p. 12.

4. The article, by Bakr Sidqi, had first appeared in the Lebanese daily *An-Nahar*.

5. Danuta Kean, "Vandals Sentenced to Read Books about Racism and Antisemitism," *Guardian*, February 7, 2017, https://www.theguardian.com/books/2017/feb/07/vandals-sentenced-to-read-books-about-racism-and-antisemitism.

6. Luigi Ferrarella, "I 30 libri sull'identità femminile per risarcire la 15enne dei Parioli," *Corriere della Sera*, September 22, 2016, https://www.corriere.it/cronache/16_settembre_23/i-30-libri-sull-identita-femminile-prostituzione-minorile-parioli-2840bf04-8101-11e6-8c4f-1739fe9f1372.shtml. The text of the sentencing (no. 266/16) in this Roman case can be found as an annex to Monica Trapani, "Prostituzione minorile e risarcimento in forma specifica del danno non patrimoniale," *Diritto Penale Contemporaneo* 2 (2017), https://archiviodpc.dirittopenaleuomo.org/d/5242-prostituzione-minorile-e-risarcimento-in-forma-specifica-del-danno-non-patrimoniale.

7. Immanuel Kant, "An Answer to the Question: What Is Enlightenment?," in *Toward Perpetual Peace and Other Writings on Politics, Peace, and History*, trans. David L. Colclasure (New Haven, CT: Yale University Press, 2006), p. 19.

8. "Address by Mr Koïchiro Matsuura, Director-General of UNESCO, on the occasion of the launch of the UN Literacy Decade at the United Nations Conference Room IV, United Nations; New York, 13 February 2003," https://unesdoc.unesco.org/ark:/48223/pf0000129380.

9. Franco Moretti, "Conjectures on World Literature," *New Left Review* 1 (January–February 2000), p. 57; included in *Distant Reading* (London: Verso, 2013), p. 48.

10. Paul Valéry, *"My Faust,"* in *Plays*, trans. David Paul and Robert Fitzgerald (New York: Pantheon Books, 1960), p. 121. Pierre Bayard devoted a witty essay to nonreading in which he refers, among others, to Valéry, a "master of non-reading." *How to Talk about Books You Haven't Read*, trans. Jeffrey Mehlman (New York: Bloomsbury, 2007), p. 15. Bayard's only apparently provocative thesis is that in the end, the "infinite reader" (p. 23), as Valéry described Anatole France, and the "absolute non-reader" (p. 3), are two extremes of which there are practically no examples: reading is, in fact, situated between the two; reading is never full ("saying we have read a book becomes essentially a form of metonymy" since "we never read more than a portion of greater or lesser length, and that portion is, in the longer or shorter term, condemned to disappear," p. 48), but neither is it ever null, either ("many books that by all appearances we haven't exert an influence on us nevertheless, as their reputations spread through society," p. xvi). When Bayard suggests that we consider that "non-reading is not just the absence of reading,"

that it is "a genuine activity, one that consists of adopting a stance in relation to the immense tide of books that protects you from drowning" (pp. 12–13), he situates himself strikingly in the wake of Moretti's work, which he does not so much as mention. Impossible, however, to think he has not read it, isn't it?

11. A history of speed in reading should be written. In the second century AD, Lucian of Samosata picked on an "ignorant book-collector" in the following terms: "To be sure you look at your books [*horas ta biblia*] with your eyes open and quite as much as you like, and you read some of them aloud with great fluency [*epitrekhōn*], keeping your eyes in advance of your lips [*to stoma*: your mouth]; but I do not consider that enough." Lucian, "The Ignorant Book-Collector," in *Works*, trans. A. M. Harmon, 8 vols. (Cambridge, MA: Harvard University Press, 1921), vol. 3, p. 177. Regarding the visual techniques used by Peter Lombard in his *Sententiae*, written around 1150, Ivan Illich writes: "In the Lombard's commentaries, key words are underlined with bright red, mercury-based lines. He ... introduces primitive quotation marks to indicate where they start and end. In the margin, references to the source from which he quotes are given.... The visual marker shifts the task ... from the inner ear to the eye.... Beyond his concern with layout, the Lombard is also aware of a new time frame to which the act of reading has been moved. He wants to lighten the burden of the student and speed up reading. He wants to decrease the need for extended leafing through the pages, and insists on chapter titles which allow the reader to find immediately what he is looking for." *In the Vineyard of the Text: A Commentary to Hugh's "Didascalicon"* (Chicago: University of Chicago Press, 1993), pp. 98–100. Although the quest for speed in reading is thus not in itself new, some historians have claimed that it took on new dimensions in the eighteenth century: Rolf Engelsing even suggests that there was a "reading revolution (*Leserevolution*): toward 1750, there was a transition from "intensive" reading (a small number of works being read and reread time and again, as was typically the case for the Bible) to "extensive" reading (readers of novels or news articles moving rapidly from one to the next). For an overview of critiques of Engelsing's hypothesis, see Leah Price, "Reading: The State of the Discipline," *Book History* 7 (2004), pp. 317–18.

12. See Stephen Best and Sharon Marcus, "Surface Reading: An Introduction," *Representations* 108.1 (Fall 2009), pp. 1–21. The authors oppose the "symptomatic reading" theorized by Louis Althusser: "a reading which might well be called '*symptomatic*' (*symptomale*), in so far as it divulges the undivulged event in the text it reads, and in the same movement relates it to *a different text*, present as a necessary absence in the first."

Reading Capital, trans. Ben Brewster (London: New Left Books, 1977), p. 28. See also: "Just reading accounts for what is in the text without construing presence as absence or affirmation as negation." Sharon Marcus, *Between Women: Friendship, Desire, and Marriage in Victorian England* (Princeton, NJ: Princeton University Press, 2007), p. 75. Eve Kosofsky Sedgwick put forward the idea of a "reparative reading": see "Paranoid Reading and Reparative Reading," in *Touching Feeling: Affect, Pedagogy, Performativity* (Durham, NC: Duke University Press, 2003), pp. 123–51. On uncritical reading, see Michael Warner, "Uncritical Reading," in *Polemic: Critical or Uncritical,* ed. Jane Gallop (London: Routledge, 2004), pp. 13–38. As for the idea of "mere reading," it appears in Paul de Man's *The Resistance to Theory* (Minneapolis: University of Minnesota Press, 1986), p. 24: "mere reading . . . prior to any theory, is able to transform critical discourse." It is surprising, to say the least, that the proponents of surface reading or mere reading are eager to distance themselves from deconstruction. Best and Marcus, for example, refer to deconstruction as one of those "demystifying protocols" that has become "superfluous" (p. 2) but end up, apparently without realizing it, using the same lexicon as one of the major thinkers of deconstruction, that is, de Man. Rodolphe Gasché recalls that Hegel already referred to "mere reading" (*blosses Lesen*), that is, silent reading, in order to defend the idea that on the contrary, poetry "must be spoken, sung, declaimed." *The Wild Card of Reading: On Paul de Man* (Cambridge, MA: Harvard University Press, 1998), p. 115.

13. Moretti, "Conjectures on World Literature," p. 53 n.19. But Moretti immediately adds that it was only a reading aimed at testing a hypothesis: "Here you don't really read the *text* anymore, but rather through the text, looking for your unit of analysis." On the mapping of "narrative markets" around 1850, see Franco Moretti, *Atlas of the European Novel 1800–1900* (London: Verso, 1999), pp. 174–76.

14. I. A. Richards, *Practical Criticism: A Study of Literary Judgment* (New York: Harcourt, Brace and Company, 1929), pp. 3–4. The expressions "closeness of reading" and "close reading" appear, for example, when Richards doubts the "closeness of his reading" of one commentator who sees only clichés in a Longfellow poem as well as when he declares, "All respectable poetry invites close reading" (pp. 164 and 203).

15. It is this same triangulation that I have tried to analyze several times as it pertains to listening: see Peter Szendy, *Listen: A History of Our Ears*, trans. Charlotte Mandell (New York: Fordham University Press, 2009); *All Ears: The Aesthetics of Espionage*, trans. Roland Végsö (New York: Fordham University Press, 2016); *Of Stigmatology: Punctuation as Experience*, trans. Jan Plug (New York: Fordham University Press, 2018).

A STRANGELY FAMILIAR VOICE

1. E. T. A. Hoffmann, "The Sandman," in *The Golden Pot and Other Tales*, trans. Ritchie Robertson (Oxford: Oxford University Press, 2009), p. 98.

2. Ibid,, p, 87.

3. Ibid., p. 93.

4. Sigmund Freud, *The Standard Edition of the Complete Psychological Works of Sigmund Freud*, trans. James Strachey, 24 vols. (London: The Hogarth Press, 1953–1974), vol. 17, p. 233.

5. Hoffmann, "The Sandman," p. 106.

6. Ibid., p. 101.

7. Ibid., p. 111.

8. Ibid., p. 112.

9. Ibid., pp. 97 and 111 (translated as "weird").

10. Ibid., p. 102.

11. Marcel Proust *On Reading*, trans. Damion Searls (London: Hesperus Press, 2011), p. 6.

THE ANAGNOST AND THE ARCHON

1. Cicero, *Letters to Atticus*, trans. E. O. Winstedt, 3 vols. (London: William Heinemann, 1919), vol. 1, p. 31.

2. Cicero, *The Letters to His Friends*, trans. W. Glynn Williams, 3 vols. (London: William Heinemann, 1958), vol. 1, p. 357.

3. See *Gargantua and Pantagruel*, chapter 21 where François Rabelais writes: "Gargantua therefore woke up at about four a.m. While he was being rubbed down, a passage of Holy Scripture was read out to him, loud and clear, with a delivery appropriate to the matter. A young page was appointed to do it: a native of Basché called Anagnostes." Rabelais, *Gargantua and Pantagruel*, trans. M. A. Screech (London: Penguin Books, 2006), p. 279. The term *anagnōstēs* comes from the Greek verb *anagignōskō*, which means to recognize and, by extension, to read. Other slavery systems, such as the one on which American plantations were based, severely repressed the possibility of slaves learning to read. Thus, the mid-nineteenth-century Code of the State of Virginia stipulates that "every assemblage of negroes for the purpose of instruction in reading or writing . . . shall be an unlawful assembly," and those who participate will "be punished with stripes." The article of the code that follows adds: "If a white person assemble with

negroes for the purpose of instructing them to read or write . . . he shall be confined in jail not exceeding six months and fined not exceeding one hundred dollars." *The Code of Virginia* (Richmond: William F. Ritchie, 1849), pp. 747–48.

4. Seneca, *Ad Lucilum epistulae morales*, trans. Richard M. Gummere (Cambridge, MA: Harvard University Press, 1970), pp. 195–97.

5. Evelyn Waugh, "The Man Who Liked Dickens," in *The Complete Stories of Evelyn Waugh* (New York: Back Bay Books, 2012), pp. 137–38. The story was published in 1933 in *Nash's Pall Mall Magazine*. Waugh reworked the story in 1934 as the end of his novel *A Handful of Dust*, changing the character's name. In the wonderful pages she devotes to "force-reading" in Victorian England, Leah Price insists on the exchange or positions or role reversal: "The servants . . . reduced to human audiobooks (standing behind their master's chair with a book during meals or hairdressing) found themselves forced, a generation later, to listen to their masters read aloud godly books. Daughters, too, were enlisted alternately to read at their fathers' sickbeds and to listen to their fathers reading family prayers." *How to Do Things with Books in Victorian Britain* (Princeton, NJ: Princeton University Press, 2012), pp. 213–14.

6. Waugh, "The Man Who Liked Dickens," p. 145.

7. Thomas A. Edison, "The Phonograph and Its Future," *North American Review* 126.262 (May–June 1878), p. 533.

8. See the remarkable pages in *A Voyage to the Moon* devoted to books that have "neither Leaves nor Letters," the reading of which requires only ears ("it was a Book made wholly for the Ears"): "So that when any Body has a mind to read in it . . . he turns the Hand to the Chapter which he desires to hear," and "imperceptible Engines" with springs take care of the rest. They can even be worn as earrings, "like a pair of Pendants." Cyrano de Bergerac, *A Voyage to the Moon*, trans. Archibald Lovell (New York: Doubleday and McClure, 1899), pp. 196–97.

9. The English translation erases the unusual adjective saying simply of the voice that it is "so audible." Immanuel Kant, *Critique of Practical Reason*, trans. Mary Gregor (Cambridge: Cambridge University Press, 1997), Ak 5:36, p. 32.

10. Jesper Svenbro, *Phrasikleia: An Anthropology of Reading in Ancient Greece*, trans. Janet Lloyd (Ithaca, NY: Cornell University Press, 1993), pp. 161–62. Svenbro recalls André Magdelain's etymological hypothesis in *La loi à Rome: Histoire d'un concept* (Paris: Les Belles Lettres, 1978), pp. 17–18 that the Latin word for law, *lex*, is the noun derived from the verb *legere*, "to read." (The law would thus first have been an "official reading out

loud.") Similarly, Svenbro suggests that we should consider *nomos*, "law" in Greek, as a noun that comes from one of the Greek verbs that means "to read," namely, *nemein*, whose main sense is "to distribute": "This is a reading aloud before an assembly, to which the content of the text is orally 'distributed'" (p. 110). The law is then a matter of voice: "Of course, the voice of the *nomos* is that which the city magistrate lends it when he recites or reads it, but it does not *belong* to this 'slave of the *nomos*,' which is what the magistrate is. [Svenbro cites Plato's *Laws*, 715d, where the archons are described as *douloi tou nomou*.] In the logic of servitude, that voice belongs to the master, that is to say, to the *nomos* itself, the master with which it is practically identified." *Phrasikleia*, p. 123. Just as the slave's voice is absorbed in the recent practice of silent reading, Socrates' "inside voice," according to Svenbro, is something new at the time: "What we might call 'the voice of conscience' is resented here as something new" (p. 162). In the *Apology*, reference is made to the "voice" (*phonē*) that, like a "daemonic" one (*daimonion*), speaks within Socrates ("a sort of voice that comes to me, and when it comes it always holds me back from what I am thinking of doing"). Plato, *Euthyphro, Apology* . . . , trans. H. N. Fowler (Cambridge, MA: Harvard University Press, 2005), 31c–d, p. 115. As for the evidence concerning the emergence of silent reading, Svenbro refers notably to a scene in Aristophanes' *Knights* where the slave Demosthenes, deep in the reading of an oracle, asks another slave to fill his cup (p. 163). Svenbro comments: "This passage, then, shows us a reader accustomed to reading silently (he is even capable of drinking and asking for a drink while doing it!) in the company of a listener who does not seem accustomed to this practice and takes the words pronounced by the reader for words read by him, which in fact they are not. The scene from the *Knights* seems particularly instructive [because] . . . it implies that the practice of silent reading was not familiar to everybody in 424 (Plato was then five years old), even if it was assumed to be so to the comedy's audience." *Phrasikleia*, pp. 163–64.

11. Plato, *Theaetetus*, in *Plato, with an English Translation*, trans. H. N. Fowler, 10 vols. (London: William Heinemann, 1917–1926), vol. 2, 143c, p. 11.

12. Plato, *Phaedrus*, trans. H. N. Fowler (New York: G. P. Putnam's Sons, 1919), 230e, p. 425.

13. Marquis de Sade, *Philosophy in the Bedroom*, in *Justine, Philosophy in the Bedroom, and Other Writings*, trans. Richard Seaver and Austryn Wainhouse (New York: Grove Press, 1965), p. 295.

14. "La mère en prescrira la lecture à sa fille" was the epigraph in the original

French. *Philosophy in the Bedroom*, p. 179. The phrase is borrowed from *La metromania*, a comedy by Alexis Piron. It would be worth lingering over other scenes of reading in Sade, such as the one in the *Juliette* when the title character is ordered to read instructions: Clairwil (the cruel libertine who oversees Juliette's education) pulls out a small brochure, and Juliette "was instructed to read it aloud. This printed document was headed by the title *Instructions to Women Admitted into the Sodality of the Friends of Crime*. From a drawer Madame de Lorsange took an envelope, opened it. 'I have kept the paper,' said she, 'for it is interesting. Listen to its contents.'" Sade inserts a footnote here ("You voluptuous women, you philosophically-minded women who deign to read us, it is once again to you this is addressed") through which he underlines and redoubles the reading scene by making it clear that Juliette is reading not only for those around her, but also for us, the readers who read her reading. Marquis de Sade, *Juliette*, trans. Austryn Wainhouse (London: Arrow Books, 1968), p. 431.

15. Jacques Lacan, "Kant with Sade," trans. James B. Swenson, Jr., *October* 51 (Winter 1989), p. 57.

16. Jacques Lacan, *The Seminar of Jacques Lacan, Book III: The Psychoses, 1955–56*, ed. Jacques-Alain Miller, trans. Russell Grigg (New York: W. W. Norton, 1997), pp. 66, 67, 68, 69, 113.

17. Ibid., p. 207.

LOVING-READING

1. Plato, *Phaedrus*, trans. H. N. Fowler (New York: G. P. Putnam's Sons, 1919), 227a, p. 413.

2. On the pederastic relationship between *erastēs* and *erōmenos* (that is, lover and loved one) in pedagogy in ancient Greece, see Henri-Irénée Marrou, "Pederasty in Classical Education," in *A History of Education in Antiquity*, trans. George Lamb (Madison: University of Wisconsin Press, 1956), pp. 26–35, and Michel Foucault, *The Use of Pleasure*, vol. 2 of *The History of Sexuality* (New York: Random House, 1990). On this relationship as a paradigm for reading, see Jesper Svenbro, *Phrasikleia: An Anthropology of Reading in Ancient Greece*, trans. Janet Lloyd (Ithaca, NY: Cornell University Press, 1993), p. 189: "Dwelling on the pederastic relationship may seem perverse in a study devoted to reading in ancient Greece.... Yet by resorting to the pederastic model the Greeks themselves tried to understand the relationship between writer and reader, apparently at a very early date. One of the earliest known definitions of the relationship between the writer

and the reader presents the writer in the role of the *erastēs* and the reader in the role of the *erōmenos*." *Phrasikleia*, p. 189.

3. Plato, *Phaedrus*, 227c, p. 415.

4. Ibid., p. 417. As Jesper Svenbro put it so well, not only was Phaedrus, historically, Lysias's *erōmenos*, "Phaedrus' reading of Lysias' speech" as staged by Plato "becomes an allegory of itself: the subject is a passionless lover . . . that coincides with the figure of the writer to whom the *erōmenos*—Phaedrus, the reader—grants the favor of his reading the speech aloud." *Phrasikleia*, p. 201.

5. Svenbro thus cites "an inscription scratched upon a black Attic kylix discovered in Gela, Sicily, and dating from 500–480 B.C." that reads as follows: "The writer of this inscription will 'bugger' the reader [*ho de graspas ton annemonta pugixei*]," *Phrasikleia*, p. 189. He compares what is written to "a series of Latin inscriptions that, though more recent, are clearly related to the Gela inscription": "the one who will write is the lover, the one who will read gets buggered [*amat qui scribet pedicatur qui leget*]"; or again, "I, who am reading, am buggered [*ego qui lego pedicor*]." Later, Svenbro describes "one red-figure Attic vase, dating from about the same period as the Gela inscription" that carries an image of "a beardless boy, draped in a cloak that reveals the contours of his body." "The boy is certainly the age of an *erōmenos* and, significantly enough, he is engaged in reading an inscription on a stele, bending forward to do so. In this position the boy's behind is much in evidence . . . the reading boy is ready to be 'buggered.' His position is that which, in iconography, suggests *katapúgōn*." *Phrasikleia*, p. 194.

6. Plato, *Phaedrus*, 228a, p. 417.

7. Ibid., 228a, p. 417.

8. Ibid., 228c, p. 417.

9. Ibid., 228e, p. 419.

10. Strato, *Musa puerilis*, *Greek Anthology*, 12.208; quoted in Svenbro, *Phrasikleia*, p. 197.

11. Plato, *Phaedrus*, 230e, p. 425.

12. In several ways, this discourse about nonlove (*aphilia*) foreshadows the pages from Sade that we will read. Consider, for example, the "Fifth Dialogue" of *Philosophy in the Bedroom*, where Dolmancé declares: "O voluptuous young women, deliver your bodies unto us as often and as much as you wish! Fuck, divert yourselves, that's the essential thing; but be quick to fly from love . . . love not at all; nor be any more concerned to make yourselves loved; to exhaust oneself in lamentation, waste in sighs, abase oneself in leering and oglings, pen billets-doux, 'tis not that which you must do; it is to fuck, to

multiply and often change your fuckers, it is above all to oppose yourselves resolutely to enslavement by any one single person, because the outcome of constant love, binding you to him, would be to prevent you from giving yourself to someone else, a cruel self-ishness which would soon become fatal to your pleasures." Marquis de Sade, *Philosophy in the Bedroom*, in *Justine, Philosophy in the Bedroom, and Other Writings*, trans. Richard Seaver and Austryn Wainhouse (New York: Grove Press, 1965), pp. 285–86. In *Juliette*, the absence of love (*aneroticism*, if you will) is the first condition laid out in the *Instructions to Women Admitted into the Sodality of the Friends of Crime* in order to reach the famous apathy that characterizes the Sadian libertine: "To attain to the apathy that must be preserved, she will…take constant care to keep her heart inaccessible to love." Marquis de Sade, *Juliette*, trans. Austryn Wainhouse (London: Arrow Books, 1968), p. 432.

13. The structure of what I am here calling a "reading point" is analogous to the "points of listening" I tried to describe in *All Ears: The Aesthetics of Espionage*, trans. Roland Végsö (New York: Fordham University Press, 2016).

14. Plato, *Phaedrus*, 234c–d, p. 435.

15. Ibid., 243d, p. 463.

16. Sade, *Philosophy in the Bedroom*, pp. 281 and 294.

17. Plato, *Phaedrus*, 243d, p. 465.

18. Ibid., 243e, p. 465.

19. Ibid., 262c–d, p. 523.

20. Ibid., 263e, p. 527.

21. Ibid., 264a, p. 529.

22. Ibid., 264c, p. 529.

23. Ibid., 263d, p. 527.

24. That the roles *can* thus be exchanged no doubt depends on the fact that they were always *exchangeable* (Phaedrus, as I underlined, is already himself split between his postures as *erōmenos* and *erastēs*). In *Masochism: Coldness and Cruelty*, after underlining the importance of these role switches ("Plato showed that Socrates appeared to be the lover but that fundamentally he was the loved one"), Gilles Deleuze suggests that "dialectic does not simply mean the free interchange of discourse, but implies transpositions or displacements of this kind, resulting in a scene being enacted simultaneously on several levels with reversals and reduplications in the allocation of roles and discourse." *Masochism: Coldness and Cruelty*, trans. Jean McNeil (New York: Zone Books, 1991), p. 22. This is what explains the importance of the Masoch-Plato couple in Deleuze's view. I prefer

to follow the Sadian paradigm because we are about to encounter the question of the categorical imperative of and in reading. Whichever way, whether one focuses on the monstrous figure of a "Plato with Sade" (as Lacan would put it), rather than that of a "Plato with Masoch," what must be avoided is the horizon that Svenbro suggests, namely, that of the pacification of reading. Such a horizon makes it impossible to think the violence in the relations of domination that inhabit any act of reading. Indeed, *Phrasikleia's* project is defined from the start in these terms: "it is legitimate to wonder whether it would not be possible to postulate a more balanced relationship between writer and reader without minimizing the specific features of each, as formulas such as "to read is to write" tend to do.... I discovered something like — yet distinct from — that more evenly balanced relationship that I was seeking. And, to my astonishment, it was in Plato's *Phaedrus* that I found it, at the point where Socrates redefines not only the relationship between lovers in a pederastic union . . . but also, through that very redefinition, the relationship of writer and reader, both of whom, as subjects, take part in one and the same search for truth." *Phasikleia*, p. 6. Svenbro returns to this in the conclusion: "What Socrates proposes in his great speech on Love, is a love that has no room for conquerors or conquered, masters or slaves, dominators or dominated. . . . I emphasize . . . that this transformation of the loving relationship into a 'Platonic love' — involving no penetration — implies the possibility of a similar transformation of the relationship between writer/reader and speaker/listener, in the sense that both these relationships are, as in the *Phaedrus*, invested by pederastic values." *Phrasikleia*, pp. 210–11. By insisting on motifs of doubling and rereading, I want to insist not on an equilibrium of forces in the practice of reading, but rather on the possible reversal or revolution of these forces.

THE NAMELESS READER

1. On the interchangeability of slave names in Plato, see the passage in the *Cratylus* where Hermogenes says to Socrates: "It seems to me that whatever name [*onoma*] you give to a thing is its right [*orthon*] name; and if you give up that name and change it for another, the later name is no less correct [*orthōs*] than the earlier, just as we change the names of our servants." *Cratylus*, in *Plato, with an English Translation*, trans. H. N. Fowler, 10 vols. (London: William Heinemann, 1917–1926), vol. 6, 384d, pp. 9–11.

2. Plato, *Theaetetus*, vol. 2, 143b–c, p. 9.

3. Ibid.

4. Ibid.

5. Ibid., p. 11.

6. Ibid.

7. Gérard Genette, *Narrative Discourse: An Essay in Method*, trans. Jane E. Lewin (Ithaca, NY: Cornell University Press, 1980), p. 237. Remember that it was Étienne Souriau who, in the preface to *L'univers filmique*, suggested the terms "diegesis" and "diegetic" to name "everything that belongs... to the story told, to the world that is supposed or proposed by the film's fiction." *L'univers filmique* (Paris: Flammarion, 1953), p. 7.

8. Jean-François Lyotard, *The Differend: Phrases in Dispute*, trans. Georges Van Den Abbeele (Minneapolis: University of Minnesota Press, 1988), p. 25.

9. Ibid.

10. Plato, *Theaetetus*, 158b-c; pp. 63–65.

11. Genette, *Narrative Discourse*, pp. 234–35.

12. Plato, *Theaetetus*, 210b, p. 257.

13. Ibid., 202c, p. 225.

14. Ibid., 203a–b, p. 227.

THE CATEGORICAL IMPERATIVE OF READING

1. Roland Barthes, "On Reading," in *The Rustle of Language*, trans. Richard Howard (Berkeley: University of California Press, 1989), p. 34.

2. "The hypothetical imperative... says only that the action is good for some *possible* or *actual* purpose" whereas "the categorical imperative... declares the action to be of itself objectively *necessary* without reference to any purpose." Immanuel Kant, *Groundwork of the Metaphysics of Morals*, trans. Mary Gregor, eds. Jens Timmermann and Mary Gregor (Cambridge: Cambridge University Press, 2012), 4:425, p. 28. We should consider another modality—requesting through prayer—that Kant uses when addressing his reader in the preface to the *Critique of Practical Reason*. As he prepares his reader to read the pages that introduce the categorical imperative, Kant does not issue a categorical demand, but instead pleads with the reader to read carefully, without leaving anything out: "I beg the reader [*ersuche ich den Leser*] not to pass lightly [*nicht mit flüchtigem Auge zu übersehen*] what is said about this concept at the conclusion of the Analytic." Immanuel Kant, *Critique of Practical Reason*, trans. Mary Gregor (Cambridge: Cambridge University Press, 1997), 5:8, p. 7. Are we, however, in fact sure that this plea does not hide an imperative? Who, which reader, could say?

3. Kant, *Groundwork*, 5:98, p. 82.

4. Marquis de Sade, *Philosophy in the Bedroom*, in *Justine, Philosophy in the Bedroom,*

and Other Writings, trans. Richard Seaver and Austryn Wainhouse (New York: Grove Press, 1965), p. 295.

5. Ibid.

6. The first edition was published in 1795 disguised by a false publication site (London, instead of Paris) and a false death announcement ("posthumous work of *Justine's* author").

7. Sade, *Philosophy in the Bedroom,* p. 339.

8. Ibid., p. 340.

9. In the original 1795 edition, pp. 180 and 213.

10. Sade, *Philosophy in the Bedroom,* pp. 349-50, ellipses in the original.

11. Roland Barthes, *Sade, Fourier, Loyola,* trans. Richard Miller (Berkeley: University of California Press, 1989), p. 168. Barthes suggests that "to sew is finally to remake a world without sewing, to return the divinely cut-up body—whose cut-up state is the source of all Sadian pleasure—to the abjection of the smooth body, the total body" (p. 169).

12. Sade, *Philosophy in the Bedroom,* p. 350.

13. Ibid., p. 366, first ellipsis in the original.

14. Ibid., p. 207.

15. Ibid., p. 255.

16. Ibid., p. 321.

17. Marquis de Sade, *Aline and Valcour or, the Philosophical Novel,* trans. Jocelyne Geneviève Barque and John Galbraith Simmons, 3 vols. (New York: Contra Mundum Press, 2019), vol. 1, p. 86. The point of sewing is, of course, to avoid what Sade describes in *Juliette,* regarding the libertine called "la Durand," as "the originality [*décousement original*] of her lewd ideas, and the wildness of their incoherence; in fine, the disorder which, established by the incredible heat of her passions, reigned throughout her entire person." Marquis de Sade, *Juliette,* trans. Austryn Wainhouse (London: Arrow Books, 1968), p. 535. For a connection between "frenzy [*déraisonnement*]" and "mindless, convulsive lasciviousness [*un décousement d'idées . . . un dévergondage*]," see also p. 1088.

18. Jacques Lacan, *The Seminar of Jacques Lacan, Book III: The Psychoses, 1955-56,* ed. Jacques-Alain Miller, trans. Russell Grigg (New York: W. W. Norton, 1997). For more on the Lacanian quilting point or button tie, see my chapter "On Restitching (Lacan vs. Derrida)" in *Of Stigmatology: Punctuation as Experience,* trans. Jan Plug (New York: Fordham University Press, 2018), pp. 30-35.

19. Sade, *Philosophy in the Bedroom*, p. 364, ellipsis in the original.

20. When he described Sade's text as a perforated piece of material, Barthes saw that as an excuse given to the reader, who would thereby be authorized not to read (everything). In other words, he suggested that the perforated texture of the text could legitimize "the ease with which the reader can 'ignore' certain pages" or certain passages. Barthes, *Sade, Fourier, Loyola*, p. 135. However, if the reader is thus pushed, so to speak, toward disobedience or inattention, if it almost becomes imperative for the reader rebel against the imperative, then, as Barthes also said, this fickle and distracted reader is already — or still — submitting to Sade's injunction, which thus appears impossible to escape from: "this ignoring [is] somehow being prepared for and legalized beforehand by the author himself, who has taken pains to produce a *perforated* text so that anyone 'skipping' the Sadian dissertations will stay within the truth of the Sadian text." Ibid. It thus seems that the reading's legality, its law or categorical imperative ("read!"), may also be the very thing that requests that one not read, the very thing that says "do not read!" (The most sadistic or Sadian form of the categorical imperative to read may be that chosen by Ulises Carrión, in that 1973 diptych I mentioned: "Dear reader. Don't read.")

21. Jacques Lacan, "Kant with Sade," trans. James B. Swenson, Jr., *October* 51 (Winter 1989), p. 74, translation emended.

22. Ibid., p. 75.

23. The epigraph in the original French edition, "La mère en prescrira la lecture à sa fille" — "The mother will prescribe its reading to her daughter" — has been omitted from the English translation.

24. Here we should compare the Sadian figure of the mother who prescribes reading with another maternal figure who is just as important for our philosophical anagnosology, the "mother's mouth" (*Muttermund*), as the "transcendental voice" (*transzendentale Stimme*) that carries the reading, analyzed by Friedrich Kittler in *Discourse Networks 1800/1900*, trans. Michael Metteer, with Chris Cullens (Stanford, CA: Stanford University Press, 1992). Kittler is mostly interested in what he calls the "metaphysics of silent reading" (*Metaphysik des leisen Lesens*) in Germany at the end of the eighteenth century and the beginning of the nineteenth. He says nothing, however, about Sade's epigraph.

25. That is notably the case for a particular type of reader, namely, translators. When Bruce Fink translates "Kant avec Sade" into English, "V . . . ée et cousue" becomes first "raped and sewn shut" and then is corrected (in the errata published here https://

brucefink.com/wp-content/uploads/2013/06/Errata-to-Complete-Ecrits.pdf) to a second version, "syphilized and sewn shut." *Écrits: The First Complete Edition in English* (New York: W. W. Norton, 2006), p. 667. James B. Swenson, Jr., in the translation used here, keeps the void of Lacan's punctuation "V . . . ed and sewn up," but adds a translator's note that suggests "violée" or "voilée."

26. Lacan, "Kant with Sade," p. 62.

27. I refer to the elliptical glossing of the graph that Lacan offers in "Kant with Sade" (pp. 62–63) and to the two pages devoted to it in his seminar *Anxiety: The Seminar of Jacques Lacan, Book 10*, ed. Jacques-Alain Miller, trans. A. R. Price (Cambridge: Polity, 2014), pp. 104–105, also from 1963, but also to Slavoj Žižek's illuminating remarks in the last chapter of *Everything You Always Wanted to Know About Lacan but Were Afraid to Ask Hitchcock*, ed. Slavoj Žižek (London: Verso, 2010).

28. Lacan, "Kant with Sade," p. 56, my emphasis.

29. Ibid., p. 58.

30. Ibid., pp. 61–62.

31. Lacan sees in the forked image of the V a visual — iconic — translation of the Latin conjunction that indicates a nonexclusive disjunction: "the V . . . whose form also evokes the union of what it divides while holding it together with a *vel*." Ibid., p. 63.

IN COURT

1. Gustave Flaubert, *Madame Bovary, A Tale of Provincial Life, Including a Complete Report of the Trial of the Author and His Complete Exoneration*, 2 vols. (Chicago: Simon P. Magee, 1904), vol. 2, appendix, p. 121. For a detailed analysis of the trial and its stakes for history and literary theory, see Dominick LaCapra's beautiful book, *Madame Bovary on Trial* (Ithaca, NY: Cornell University Press, 1982).

2. Ibid., pp. 33, 64–65, 80.

3. Ibid., p. 4.

4. "Plaidoirie de Maurice Garçon," in *L'affaire Sade: Compte-rendu exact du procès intenté* (Paris: Jean-Jacques Pauvert, 1957), p. 94. Garçon declares, as he began his speech for the defense, that "common opinion would have the Marquis de Sade condemned without a debate. Yet few of those who speak of them have read his works. They adjudicate without knowing, relying on what they have been told, which is the most dangerous method for judges. If I claimed they have not read a single line, perhaps I would be going too far. A few particularly indecent passages have long circulated in manuscripts passed

hand to hand among students in middle or high school." Ibid., pp. 88–89. Even if he thus seems to regret that those who condemn or defend Sade have not read his works, Garçon does not himself read any more than they do (he barely quotes a few lines lifted here or there), whereas for example he quotes a flagellation scene in Proust at length. The verdict pronounced on the January, 10, 1957, condemned Jean-Jacques Pauvert to pay a fine of 200,000 francs and ordered the "destruction of the seized works." It was overthrown by the court of appeal March 12, 1958.

5. Flaubert, *Madame Bovary*, vol. 2, appendix, p. 4.

6. Ibid., p. 10.

7. Ibid.

8. Ibid., p. 32.

9. Ibid., p. 61.

10. Ibid.

11. Ibid., p. 66.

12. Ibid., p. 67.

13. Ibid., p. 111.

14. Ibid., pp. 111–12.

READING GENDERS

1. Italo Calvino, *If on a Winter's Night a Traveler*, trans. William Weaver (London: Vintage, 1998), p. 3.

2. Marcel Proust, *Swann's Way*, trans. Lydia Davis (New York: Penguin Classics, 2004), p. 3.

3. Italo Calvino, "Se una notte d'inverno un narratore," *Alfabeta*, December 1979 (Calvino responding to Angelo Guglielmi).

4. Jacques Derrida and Derek Attridge, "'This Strange Institution Called Literature': An Interview with Jacques Derrida," trans. Geoffrey Bennington and Rachel Bowlby, in *Acts of Literature*, ed. Derek Attridge (New York: Routledge, 1992), p. 74.

5. Lucian of Samosata, "A Portrait Study," in *The Works of Lucian of Samosata: Complete with Exceptions Specified in the Preface*, trans. H. W. Fowler and F. G. Fowler, 4 vols. (Oxford: Clarendon Press of Oxford University Press, 1905), vol. 3, p. 17.

6. Christine de Pizan, *The Book of the City of Ladies*, trans. Earl Jeffrey Richards (New York: Persea Books, 1982), p.153. When Christine de Pizan asks about a book of spells (wrongly) attributed to Albert the Great and known as *Secreta mulierum* (The secret of

women), "Reason" reminds her of the warning at the beginning of the book that "every man who read the work to a woman or gave it to a woman to read" risked being "excommunicated" (p. 22). And why such a threat? Because "the man who wrote it knew that if women read it or heard it read aloud, they would know it was lies, would contradict it, and make fun of it" (pp. 22–23).

7. Pierre Sylvain Maréchal, *Projet d'une loi portant défense d'apprendre à lire aux femmes* (Paris: Massé, 1801), pp. 4 and 49. Maréchal goes so far as to ground the prohibition of reading for women on what he claims is sexual equality: "The two sexes are perfectly equal; that is to say that they are each perfect in what constitutes them . . . the only thing uglier in the world than a man acting like a woman is a woman acting like a man" (pp. v–vi).

8. For a good general introduction to the place of women in reading, see Belinda Jack, *The Woman Reader* (New Haven, CT: Yale University Press, 2012), which goes all the way back to high antiquity, identifying a few rare women scribes in Mesopotamia.

9. Johann Paul Friedrich Richter, "Review of Madame de Stael's *Allemagne*," *Fraser's Magazine for Town and Country* 1 (February–July 1830), p. 28. Reprised as "spiritual Amazon" on p. 413.

10. Ibid., p. 410.

11. Calvino, *If on a Winter's Night a Traveler*, p. 142. Note that Weaver here translates *Lettore*, a male reader, as "Reader" and the feminine form of reader, *Lettrice*, as "lady Reader." Elsewhere he uses "Reader"/"Other Reader" to mark the distinction, which in Italian is explicitly gendered.

12. Ibid.

13. Ibid., p. 145.

14. Ibid., p. 146.

15. Ibid.

16. Ibid., p. 147.

17. Ibid.

18. Calvino, "Se una notte d'inverno un narratore," p. 369.

19. Calvino, *If on a Winter's Night a Traveler*, p. 176, translation emended.

20. I must here refer to memorable pages of Gilles Deleuze's exchange with Claire Parnet: "Verbs in the infinitive are limitless becomings" and "infinitive-becomings have no subject: they refer only to an 'it' of the event (it is raining). . . . If the infinitives . . . are events, it is because there is a part of them which their accomplishment is not enough to realize, a becoming in itself which constantly both awaits us and precedes us, like a third

person of the infinitive, a fourth person singular." *Dialogues*, trans. Hugh Tomlinson and Barbara Habberjam (New York: Columbia University Press, 1987), pp. 64–65.

21. Calvino, *If on a Winter's Night a Traveler*, p. 29.

22. Ibid., p. 32.

23. Ibid.

24. Ibid.

25. Ibid., p. 68.

26. Ibid., p. 72.

27. Ibid., p. 140.

28. There are innumerable examples. There are many systolic moments, such as this one: "Would you like . . . to establish that exclusive bond, that communion of inner rhythm, that is achieved through a book's being read at the same time by two people, as you thought possible with Ludmilla" (p. 125)? Or again: "You are in bed together, you two Readers. So the moment has come to address you in the second person plural, a very serious operation, because it is tantamount to considering the two of you a single subject" (p. 154). Note, however, that the diastolic sentence follows immediately: "what you are doing is very beautiful, but grammatically it doesn't change a thing. At the moment when you most appear to be a united *voi*, a second person plural, you are two *tu's*, more separate and circumscribed than before" (p. 154). The diastole is particularly clear in the following passage from that same chapter seven: "Reading is solitude. To you Ludmilla appears protected by the valves of the open book like an oyster in its shell. . . . One reads alone, even in another's presence. But what, then, are you looking for here? Would you like to penetrate her shell, insinuating yourself among the pages of the books she is reading? Or does the relationship between one Reader and the Other Reader remain that of two separate shells, which can communicate only through partial confrontations of two exclusive experiences?" (p. 147). The ultimate systole-diastole of the twelfth and last chapter (which we are about to read) is announced in the final pages of chapter seven: "Tomorrow, Reader and Other Reader, if you are together, if you lie down in the same bed like a settled couple, each will turn on the lamp at the side of the bed and sink into his or her book" (pp. 156–57).

29. Ibid., p. 260.

READING, BINDING, UNBINDING

1. Søren Kierkegaard, *Stages on Life's Way*, trans. Howard V. Hong and Edna H. Hong (Princeton, NJ: Princeton University Press, 1989), p. 4.

2. Ibid., p. 485.

3. Martin Heidegger, "What Is Called Reading?," trans. John Sallis, in Hugh J. Silverman and Don Ihde, eds., *Hermeneutics and Deconstruction* (Albany: SUNY University Press, 1985), p. viii; "Was heisst lesen?," in Heidegger, *Aus der Erfahrung des Denkens, 1910–1976* (Frankfurt am Main: Klostermann, 1983), p. 111.

4. Martin Heidegger, *What Is Called Thinking?*, trans. Fred. D. Weick and J. Glenn Gray (New York: Harper & Row, 1968), p. 208.

5. Martin Heidegger, "Language in the Poem," in *On The Way to Language*, trans. Peter D. Hertz (New York: Harper & Row, 1971), pp. 160–61. See Jacques Derrida's commentary on this passage: "It will be said of the poetic place that only a leap could, with one blow [*coup*], one glance [*coup d'oeil*], open access to it. This leaping, sometimes elliptical and discontinuous approach is what literary critics, philologists, and philosophers reproach Heidegger for: he supposedly jumps arbitrarily in the middle of a poem, from one verse to another, from one poem to another without warning, without methodological caution. Heidegger knows this, he takes it on: blows, leaps, jumps, that's the rhythm and regime of this 'reading' which does something other than 'to read' and which remains simultaneously so slow, winding, cautious, lingering, retracing its steps, etc." *Geschlecht III: Sex, Race, Nation, Humanity*, ed. Geoffrey Bennington, Katie Chenoweth, and Rodrigo Therezo, trans. Katie Chenoweth and Rodrigo Therezo (Chicago: University of Chicago Press, 2020), p. 15. Warm thanks to David Mullins for drawing my attention to these Heideggerian leaps during our discussions in my seminar on reading at Brown University in 2020. (See his admirable dissertation on the right to singularity, in which he develops the idea of a *Blitzlesen*, a "lightning reading.")

6. Maurice Blanchot, "Reading," in *The Space of Literature*, trans. Ann Smock (Lincoln: University of Nebraska Press, 1982), pp. 190–96. Note that *lire* in French is the infinitive of the verb — not "reading," but "to read."

7. This was a comment on Marguerite Duras's novel *Détruire dit-elle*. See Maurice Blanchot, "Destroy," in *Friendship*, trans. Elizabeth Rottenberg (Stanford, CA: Stanford University Press, 1997), p. 114.

8. Blanchot, "Reading," pp. 192–93. See also: "It would seem, then, that to read is not to write the book again, but to allow the book to *be*: written — this time all by itself, without the intermediary of the writer, without anyone's writing it. The reader does not add himself to the book, but tends primarily to relieve it of an author" (p. 192).

9. Ibid., p. 193.

10. Ibid., p. 195.

11. It is hard here not to think of what Jacques Derrida will write thirty years later about the "yes" as "originary word," which "undoubtedly belongs to language" (it is, after all, a word like any other), but which is also "implicated by all the other words whose source it figures" (because one has to have assented to language in order to speak it): "It *causes* to be and *lets* be everything that can be said." Jacques Derrida, *Psyche: Inventions of the Other*, ed. and trans. Peggy Kamuf and Elizabeth Rottenberg, 2 vols. (Stanford, CA: Stanford University Press, 2008), vol. 2, pp. 236–37. In the end, this Blanchotian oscillation between doing and letting situates this "yes" beyond the scope of any speech-act theory. (The "yes" pronouncing marriage was J. L. Austin's prime example of what he was the first to describe as "speech acts.") The "yes," as an "absolute performative" and "archi-engagement," "is not, strictly speaking, an act; it is not assignable to any subject or to any object" (ibid., pp. 238–89).

12. Blanchot, "Reading," p. 190. The ellipsis here is mine.

13. Ibid., p. 194.

14. In Hofmannsthal, Death itself pronounces these words at the very end of *Death and the Fool*, a drama in one act, written in in 1893. As Claudio, the protagonist, has just fallen unconscious at its feet, Death moves away slowly, declaring: "How wonderful these humans are indeed, / ... And what was never writ, they read." Hugo von Hofmannsthal, *Death and the Fool*, trans. Elizabeth Walter (Boston: Richard G. Badger, 1914), p. 45.

15. Blanchot, "Reading," p. 193, my emphasis.

16. Roland Barthes conceives of a "rereading ... suggested at the outset." As he put it in "a deliberate contradiction in terms, we *immediately* reread the text." Roland Barthes, "How Many Readings?," in *S/Z*, trans. Richard Miller (Malden, UK: Blackwell, 1990), p. 16.

17. Michel de Certeau, "Reading as Poaching," in *The Practice of Everyday Life*, trans. Steven Rendall (Berkeley: University of California Press, 1988), p. 169.

18. Ibid.

19. Ibid.

20. Ibid., p. 176.

21. Ibid.

22. Ibid., pp. 175–76.

23. Michel de Certeau, "Absolute Reading," chapter 5 in *The Mystic Fable, Volume Two: The Sixteenth and Seventeenth Centuries*, trans. Michael B. Smith (Chicago: University of Chicago Press, 2015), p. 120.

24. Ibid., p. 131.

25. Ibid.

26. Ibid., p. 121.

27. De Certeau, "Reading as Poaching," p. 173.

28. Ibid., pp. 166–67 and 171; "Absolute Reading," p. 121. In his course from 1981–1982, Michel Foucault devotes important sections to reading as a "practice of the self" or as a way of "rejoining oneself." He refers in particular to Seneca's advice about reading: "Actually, the advice given, with regard to reading at least, arises from a common practice in Antiquity and which the principles of philosophical reading take up, but without fundamentally changing them. That is to say, first, read few books; read few authors; read few works; within these works, read a few passages; chose passages considered to be important and sufficient." *Hermeneutics of the Subject, Lectures at the Collège de France, 1981–1982*, trans. Graham Burchell (New York: Palgrave Macmillan, 2005), pp. 331, 333, 355. Note the recommendation of moderation, along with encouragement to meditative slowness described as a form of digestion. (See, for example, the second letter from Seneca to Lucilius: "after you have run over many thoughts, select one to be thoroughly digested [*concoquas*] that day." Seneca, *Ad Lucilum epistulae morales*, trans. Richard M. Gummere (Cambridge, MA: Harvard University Press, 1970), p. 9. They presuppose a reading scene that is already triangulated between the reader (who pronounces the imperative here), the readee, and the text. Foucault indeed continues thus: "Or again, as was the case for Seneca with Lucilius, for example, there is the practice of noting down quotations from this or that author and then sending them to a correspondent, saying to him: Here is an important or interesting phrase; I am sending it to you; reflect, meditate on it, etcetera." Foucault, *Hermeneutics of the Subject*, p. 356.

29. De Certeau, "Reading as Poaching," p. 173.

30. Ibid., pp. 173–74.

31. "A genuine reading never puts the genuine book into question. But neither does it submit to the 'text.' Only the nonliterary book is presented as a tightly woven net of determined significations, a set of real affirmations. Before being read by anyone, the nonliterary book has already been read by all, and it is this prior reading that guarantees it a solid existence. But the book which has its origin in art has no guarantee

in the world, and when it is read, it has never been read before." Blanchot, *The Space of Literature*, p. 194.

32. See Peter Szendy, *Prophecies of Leviathan: Reading Past Melville*, trans. Gil Anidjar (New York: Fordham University Press, 2010), of which this book is, in many ways, an extension.

THE READING MACHINE

1. Horst Bredekamp, "Thomas Hobbes's Visual Strategies," in *The Cambridge Companion to Hobbes's Leviathan*, ed. Patricia Springborg (Cambridge: Cambridge University Press, 2007), p. 40.

2. Thomas Hobbes, introduction to *Leviathan* (New York: Oxford University Press, 1998), p. 7.

3. On the classical figure of effiction, which involves fashioning the form of a body with words, see my *Phantom Limbs: On Musical Bodies*, trans. Will Bishop (New York: Fordham University Press, 2015).

4. Few commentators have highlighted the importance of this theme in *Leviathan*. One exception, although from a very different perspective from the one adopted here, is Gary Shapiro, "Reading and Writing in the Text of Hobbes' Leviathan," *Journal of the History of Philosophy* 18.2 (April 1980), pp. 147–57.

5. Hobbes, introduction to *Leviathan*, pp. 7–8.

6. Giorgio Agamben mentions "the existence of a manuscript copy on parchment, which Hobbes had prepared for Charles II and in which the image on the frontispiece presents some important differences": "here the tiny men that form the sovereign's body are turned not toward the head of the sovereign as in the book, but toward the reader, that is, toward the sovereign for whom the manuscript was intended." *Stasis: Civil War as a Political Paradigm* (Homo Sacer II, 2), trans. Nicholas Heron (Edinburgh: Edinburgh University Press, 2015), p. 30. Agamben adds that "there is not really a contrast between the two frontispieces, because in both cases the subjects direct their gaze toward the sovereign" (ibid.).

7. Hobbes, *Leviathan*, part 1, chapter 4, p. 24.

8. Ibid.

9. Ibid., part 1, chapter 5, p. 27.

10. Ibid., p. 28.

11. Ibid., p. 27.

12. Ibid., p. 28.

13. Ibid., "A Review and Conclusion," pp. 468–74.

14. Ibid., p. 475.

15. Ibid., part 1, chapter 16, p. 107.

16. Ibid., p. 109.

17. Ibid., "A Review and Conclusion," p. 473.

18. Ibid., part 3, chapter 32, p. 247, my emphasis.

19. Ibid.

20. Ibid., part 3, chapter 36, p. 281.

21. Ibid., p. 282, my emphasis.

22. Ibid.

FAST READING

1. Paul Valéry, *Cahiers/Notebooks 2*, ed. Brian Stimpson, trans. Robert Pickering et al (Bern: Peter Lang, 2000), p. 265.

2. Ibid., p. 269.

3. Ibid., p. 282.

4. Ibid., p. 268.

5. Ibid., p. 267.

6. Seneca, *Ad Lucilum epistulae morales*, trans. Richard M. Gummere (Cambridge, MA: Harvard University Press, 1970), p. 9.

7. William of Saint-Thierry, *The Golden Epistle: A Letter to the Brethren at Mont Dieu*, trans. Theodore Berkeley (Spencer, MA: Cistercian Publications, 1971), p. 52

8. Arthur Schopenhauer, *The World as Will and Representation*, trans. E. F. J. Payne, 2 vols. (New York: Dover, 1969), vol. 1, p. xiii.

9. Friedrich Nietzsche, *Daybreak: Thoughts on the Prejudices of Morality*, trans. R. J. Hollingdale (Cambridge: Cambridge University Press, 1997), p. 5.

10. Ibid.

11. Paul Valéry, *"My Faust,"* in *The Collected Works of Paul Valéry, Volume 3: Plays*, trans. David Paul and Robert Fitzgerald (New York: Pantheon Books, 1960), p. 42, translation emended.

12. Johann Wolfgang von Goethe, *Faust I & II*, trans. Stuart Atkins (Princeton, NJ: Princeton University Press, 2014), verse 46, p. 3.

13. Goethe, *Faust I*, verses 386–90, p. 13.

14. See Franco Moretti, *Distant Reading* (London: Verso, 2013).

15. Goethe, *Faust I*, verses 2065–66, p. 52.

16. Goethe, *Faust II*, verses 638 and 6850, pp. 175 and 176.

17. Ibid., verses 7034–35, p. 180.

18. Ibid., verse 6993, p. 179.

19. There are several mentions in the *Notebooks* of a "Faust III." See, for example, "A 3rd Faust. All magic devalued. . . . Popularization of powers and marvels. The fool can fly." *Cahiers/Notebooks 2*, p. 429. Or "Faust III . . . take the Faust theme and situate it in the present World . . . bring out the notion of *acceleration*, fatal characteristic of the modern" (ibid., p. 442).

20. On the subject of the quotation marks, Valéry notes: "I place words between *quotation marks* less to highlight than to *accuse*—They render suspect. Or else I confer on the meaning an assumption about the use made of it by certain individuals. I do not assume responsibility—for the term—etc. Quotations marks=provisional" (ibid., p. 505). Jean-Michel Rey quite rightly underlines the "idea evoked in *'My Faust'*: that a book title can be stolen *before* having been produced." Paul Valéry, *L'aventure d'une œuvre* (Paris: Seuil, 1991), p. 29.

21. Valéry, *"My Faust,"* p. 3, translation emended.

22. Michel de Montaigne, *The Complete Essays*, trans. M. A. Screech (London: Penguin Books, 1993), p. lxiii.

23. Charles Baudelaire, *The Flowers of Evil*, trans. James McGowan (Oxford: Oxford University Press, 2008), p. 7.

24. Valéry, *"My Faust,"* p. 138. Note that translation of the character's name has been emended to stay closer to the original.

25. Ibid., p.3.

26. Ibid., p. 29.

27. Ibid., pp. 32–34.

28. Ibid., pp. 13–14, translation emended.

29. Boredom was already present in Goethe's *Faust I*, where the theater director in the prologue hypothesizes that some spectators will come "driven by boredom" (verse 113, p. 4), and in *Faust II*, Mephistopheles is "bore[d]" just before the balloon trip that will carry him to the Classical Walpurgisnight after a flyover of a whole section of the world library (verse 6958, p. 178).

30. Valéry, *"My Faust,"* p. 52.

31. "At a very early stage I was struck and exasperated by the periodical nature of 'life'—in its framework of orbits and seasons—of frequent and useless repetition.... 'My Faust' is the man who is only too aware of this cyclical malady, and this awareness constantly rubs his nose in this cyclomania essentially defining us." Valéry, *Cahiers/ Notebooks*, 2, p. 531.

32. Valéry, *"My Faust,"* p. 79.

33. Ibid., pp. 79–80.

34. Ibid., p. 108.

35. Some have thought of Anglo-Saxon close reading as a descendant of the French *explication de texte* (suggested, for example, by Michael Hancher, "Re: Search and Close Reading," in Mathew K. Gold and Lauren F. Klein, eds., *Debates in the Digital Humanities* (Minneapolis: University of Minnesota Press, 2016), p. 120. In the context of Valéry's anagnosology, it may be worth remembering what Gustave Lanson said when, in a section of his *Méthodes de l'histoire littéraire* bearing the title "Quelques mots sur l'explication de textes," he offers a late codification of a practice that already had a long educational history (his work was published in 1925): "Too many people . . . are used to reading only very fast, the way one reads a newspaper or a novel [sic], to scan rather than read. Others call 'reading' their habit of dreaming on the pages of a book [it's as though one were stumbling on the Student from *"My Faust"* before he fell asleep], and sometimes imagine finding there . . . what was only ever the play of their imagination or the emotion of their heart. . . . The exercise of an *explication* aims to . . . create in students the habit of reading literary texts attentively and interpreting them faithfully" (p. 40).

36. See, for instance, Anne Ubersfeld, *"Lust* ou la voix de l'autre," *Littérature* 56 (1984), p. 56; Julia Peslier, "Faust à l'épreuve du médiéval: Mémoires du Faust-Phénix chez Pessoa et Valéry, Boulgakov et Mann," *Littérature* 148 (2007), p. 90.

37. Louis Sébastien Le Nain de Tillemont, *Mémoires pour servir à l'histoire ecclésiastique des six premiers siècles . . .* (Paris: Charles Robustel, 1701), vol. 12, p. 80.

38. Ibid., pp. 12 and 14–15.

39. Ibid., p. 16.

40. "Le subjonctif exprime l'action d'une manière dépendante, subordonnée, incertaine, conditionnelle." César Chesneau Dumarsais, *Mélanges de grammaire, de philosophie, etc. tirés de l'Encyclopédie*, in *Œuvres* (Paris: Pougin, 1791), vol. 4, p. 342; see also the article s.v. *conjonctif* (conjunctive): "the indicative affirms directly and does not

suppose anything; in contrast, the endings of the subjunctive are always subordinate to an indicative that is either explicitly expressed or implicit" (p. 330).

41. In a tribute to Hélène Cixous, Jacques Derrida devotes crucial pages to the subjunctive, to the "subjunctive mood," and to the "time to come." Jacques Derrida, *H. C. for Life, That Is to Say . . .* , trans. Laurent Milesi and Stefan Herbrechter (Stanford, CA: Stanford University Press, 2006), p. 61. Prowling, as he puts it, "around the relationships between subjunctivity and subjectivity, these two moods or modes of subjugation, subjection, and subordination," he tries to prove that "the subjunctive is mightier, from the subordinate clause, than the ontological main clause." (pp. 104–105). Mightier, but with a different might, that of a performative that precedes and conditions any indicative, that allows the indicative to arrive, like Blanchot's "light, innocent, yes of reading." (Indeed, Derrida evokes a "poetics of reading.") This remarkable meditation on the "originary subjunctive" (p. 70) is also tightly interwoven with references to the "absolute speed" (p. 72) that drives it, or rather to the "differential of speed" that it seems to be (since "there is no *essence* of speed . . . outside this differential") (p. 73).

42. Valéry, *"My Faust,"* p. 121.

READERS' CORRESPONDENCE

1. The illustration here shows the back cover of the French publication: László Krasznahorkai, *La venue d'Isaïe*, trans. Joëlle Dufeuilly (Paris: Cambourakis, 2013). This was published separately from the novel in this particular format, encouraging the postal analysis offered here. In English, it is published as "Isaiah Has Come" at the end of the volume containing *War and War*, trans. George Szirtes (New York: New Directions, 2006).

2. In French, this chapter plays on the many possible readings of its title: "Courrier des lecteurs." In an antiquated meaning, *courrier* refers to a courier, as in English. In contemporary French, however, it refers to the correspondence itself—mail in general. Furthermore, the entire phrase, *courrier des lecteurs*, is the standard rubric for "letters to the editor" or "readers' correspondence" in news publications—Trans.

3. Krasznahorkai, *War and War*, p. 204.

4. Ibid.

5. Krasznahorkai, "Isaiah Has Come," p. 259.

6. Ibid.

7. In recent correspondence in which we were discussing matters of punctuation, László told me that he is often asked why he avoids periods. His preferred response,

deliberately irritating, as he told it, is the following: "Only God can put a period" (*a pontot csak a Jóisten teheti le*). And he added, in his enigmatic fashion: "but it doesn't matter if there is a period or not" (*és most mindegy, hogy van, vagy nincs*).

8. Krasznahorkai, "Isaiah Has Come," p. 269.

9. Ibid.

10. In classical Greek, a contraction that makes one word out of two. Crasis also occurs in modern languages such as French and Portuguese. In French, it "involves the grammaticalization of two individual lexical items into one," whereas in classical Greek, it is "the orthographic representation of the encliticization and the vowel reduction of one grammatical form with another." They differ in that the Greek involves "two grammatical words and a single phonological word," while the French involves "a single phonological word and grammatical word." See *Wikipedia*, s.v. "Crasis," https://en.wikipedia.org/wiki/Crasis.

11. Krasznahorkai, "Isaiah Has Come," p. 270.

12. László Krasznahorkai, *Satantango*, trans. George Szirtes and Ottilie Mulzet (New York: New Directions, 2020), p. 213.

13. László Krasznahorkai, *Animalinside*, trans. Ottilie Mulzet (New York: New Directions, 2010), p. 12.

14. Ibid., p. 11.

15. Krasznahorkai, "Isaiah Has Come," p. 257.

16. Krasznahorkai, *War and War*, p. 23.

17. Ibid.

18. Ibid., p. 48.

19. Ibid., p. 19.

20. Ibid., p. 81.

21. Ibid., pp. 19, 89, 93, 249.

22. Ibid., p. 220.

23. Ibid., p. 84.

24. Ibid., pp. 93, 84.

25. Ibid., p. 83.

26. Ibid., p. 93.

27. Ibid., p. 212.

28. Ibid., p. 203.

29. Ibid., p. 109.

30. Ibid., p. 153.

31. Immanuel Kant, "Perpetual Peace: A Philosophical Sketch," trans. H. B. Nisbet, in *Political Writings*, ed. Hans Reiss (Cambridge: Cambridge University Press, 1991), p. 93.

32. Krasznahorkai, *War and War*, p. 203.

33. Ibid., my emphasis.

34. Ibid.

35. Ibid., p. 224.

36. Ibid., p. 239.

37. Ibid.

38. Ibid.

39. Ibid., p. 234.

40. Ibid.

41. Ibid., p. 247.

42. Ibid., p. 248.

43. Ibid., p. 250.

44. Ibid., pp. 250–51.

45. Ibid., p. 251.

46. In 2014, the museum (the Hallen für neue Kunst, founded by Urs Raussmüller) was forced to move to Basel, but it still houses Mario Merz's igloo.

47. Ibid., p. 253.

48. When you go on Google Street View to number 23 Baumgartenstrasse in Schaffhausen (try, you will see), you can still see the said plaque. Since 2015, when the French translation of *War and War* was published in paperback by Babel, the site https://guerreetguerre.wordpress.com (which, as we will see, also prolongs the narrative) provides the following information in French, in the form of another address to the reader: "Dear reader, I can understand that you want to see György Korin's last sentence with you own eyes. Until now, you could have done so following the instructions given on the inside cover of *War and War*. From now on, you will have to go to Basel if you want to know what Korin had engraved on the plaque because the plaque, as well as Mario Merz's igloo where Korin would have liked his life to end, are now in the Raussmüller in Basel. If you feel like pursuing the adventure a little further, to see the place where Korin's trajectory, beyond the last page of the novel, ended in reality, then, before going, or after having been to Basel, follow the instructions of *War and War* and go to the old Hallen für neue Kunst in Schaffhausen. To the left of the entrance door, you can see and one will no

doubt for a long time be able to see, where the plaque was. And the place where Korin ended his days. Have a good trip! László Krasznahorkai."

49. "Not Found. The requested URL / was not found on this server." warandwar. com.

50. Krasznahorkai, *War and War*, p. 234. It would be better to imagine something along the lines of what Jean-Christophe Bailly proposes in his beautiful essay on the reader's task when he evokes the "breeze" of a sentence. "La tâche du lecteur," in *Panoramiques* (Paris: Bourgois, 2000), p. 42.

51. Maurice Blanchot, "Reading," in *The Space of Literature,* trans. Ann Smock (Lincoln: University of Nebraska Press 1982), p. 197. "Infraslim" (*inframince*) is a term borrowed from Marcel Duchamp, who makes the following comparison: "When the tobacco smoke also smells of the mouth which exhales it, the two odors are married by the infraslim." *The Essential Writings of Marcel Duchamp*, ed. Michel Sanouillet and Elmer Peterson (London: Thames and Hudson, 1975), p. 194.

52. In an interview, Krasznahorkai talks about those sinuous meandering sentences so familiar to his readers (*War and War* is composed of 152 sentences, some of which are ten pages long): "For me a sentence — each sentence — is a matter of life and death; I can work on a sentence for several weeks, and I do so in my head, not in front of a sheet of paper, and I only write it down when it is ready" ("... lélegzetre írom ezeket a mondatokat") interview by Eszter Rádai, in *Élet és irodalom*, January 28, 2000, in Zoltán Hafner, ed., *Krasznahorkai beszélgetések* (Budapest: Széphalom Könyvműhely, 2003), p. 65.

53. Krasznahorkai, *War and War*, p. 196.

54. Ibid., p. 198.

55. Ibid., p. 200.

56. Ibid., p. 202.

57. Ibid., pp. 200–201.

58. Ibid., p. 200.

59. I had suggested the term *dis-contraction* to describe what happens to Pip, the character in *Moby Dick*, in one of the many allegories of reading in Melville's great novel, to name the systole-diastole that affects the punctuating points. *Prophecies of Leviathan: Reading Past Melville*, trans. Gil Anidjar (New York: Fordham University Press, 2010), p. 58. I took up the term again in *Of Stigmatology: Punctuation as Experience*, trans. Jan Plug (New York: Fordham University Press, 2018), pp. 9, 68, 74.

60. Hobbes, "A Review and Conclusion," p. 473.

61. László Krasznahorkai, "On Velocity," in *The World Goes On*, trans. John Bakti, Ottilie Mulzet, and George Szirtes (New York: New Directions, 2017), p. 11.

62. Ibid., p. 13.

63. Ibid., p. 11. In the version published in *Jelenkor* 52.7–8 (July–August 2009), pp. 715–17, the fictional place names Monowitz, Schuhkammer, and Kleiderkammer are replaced with Twelfth Avenue and Avenue A, as though the story took place in New York, like Korin's adventures in *War and War*.

64. Krasznahorkai, "On Velocity," p. 12.

65. Ibid., pp. 13–14.

66. Ibid., p. 95: "the manuscript's superbly honed [*leheletfinom:* literally "breath-thin"] and supple sentences." Or p. 174: where the author's "technique" for ceaselessly modulating the sentences of the manuscript is described as "delicate, light as a feather [*leheletfinom*]."

67. Ibid., "On Velocity," p. 13.

ARCHEREADING

1. Recalling the biblical sense of jubilee ("in every seventh year a lesser, and in every seven times seventh, or forty ninth, a greater, Jubilee-, Intercalary-, Indulgence-, Sab-bath-, or Trumpet-year occurred, in which one lived without debts, without sowing and laboring, and without slavery"), Jean Paul writes: "I make a sufficiently happy applica-tion, as it seems to me, of this title, Jubilee, to my historical chapters, which conduct the business-man and the business-woman round and round in an easy cycle or circle full of free Sabbath-, Indulgence-, Trumpet-, and Jubilee-hours, in which both have neither to sow nor to pay, but only to reap and to rest; for I am the only one who, like the bowed and crooked-up drudge of a ploughman, stand at my writing-table, and see sowing-machines, and debts of honor, and manacles, before and on me." *Titan: A Romance*, trans. Charles T. Brooks, 2 vols. (Boston: Ticknor and Fields, 1862), vol. 1, pp. 57–58.

2. Thomas Hobbes, "A Review and Conclusion," in *Leviathan* (New York: Oxford University Press, 1998), p. 473.

3. Hugo von Hofmannsthal, *Death and the Fool: A Drama in One Act*, trans. Elisabeth Walter (Boston: R. G. Badger, 1914), p. 45.

4. Walter Benjamin, "Paralipomena to 'On the Concept of History,'" trans. Edmund Jephcott and Howard Eiland, in *Walter Benjamin: Selected Writings, Volume 4, 1938–1940*, eds. Howard Eiland and Michael W. Jennings (Cambridge, MA: Belknap Press of Harvard

University Press, 2003), p. 405. The "recent author" to whom Benjamin refers is André Monglond, *Le préromantisme français*, 2 vols. (Grenoble: Arthaud, 1930), vol. 1, p. xiii.

5. Walter Benjamin, "On the Mimetic Faculty," trans. Edmund Jephcott, in *Walter Benjamin: Selected Writings, Volume 2, 1927–1934*, eds. Michael W. Jennings, Howard Eiland, and Gary Smith (Cambridge, MA: Belknap Press of Harvard University Press, 1999), p. 722.

6. The archereading I am trying to conceptualize here has nothing to do with the idea of an "archereader" Michael Riffaterre once put forward, defining it as a sort of "sum of readings" (*somme de lectures*). *Essais de stylistique structurale* (Paris: Flammarion, 1971), p. 46. It comes closer to what Michel Lisse named thus, although I would not follow him in being concerned to "free reading from the yoke of listening," from submission to "what can be heard." *L'expérience de la lecture, 2: Le glissement* (Paris: Galilée, 2001), pp. 13, 15, 18, 189. Furthermore, Lisse posits that what he calls "archreading" and Derrida's "arche-writing" are simply complementary: he can simply say that "to arche-writing there corresponds an archereading" (à l'archi-écriture correspond une archilecture, p. 189), as though the latter were simply the receptive side of the former. Instead, I understand the relation to be characterized by tension and tangentiality.

7. Walter Benjamin, "Doctrine of the Similar," trans. Michael Jennings, in *Selected Writings, Volume 2, 1927–1934*, p. 697.

8. Ibid.

9. Blaise Pascal, *Pensées*, trans. W. F. Trotter (New York: E. P. Dutton, 1958), no. 69, p. 16. This sentence corresponds to fragment no. 41 in the Lafuma edition, *Pensées* (Paris: Éditions du Luxembourg, 1951). See also the facsimile reproduction of the original fragment on the excellent site "Fragment *Vanité* no. 28," *Pensées de Blaise Pascal*, penseesdepascal.fr, http://www.penseesdepascal.fr/Vanite/Vanite28-diplomatique.php, where as a reader, you can have the strange experience of a sort of stuttering repetition between Pascal's handwriting and the handwriting of his secretary: "Quand on lit trp Viste ou quand on lit trop viste ou trop doucement on entend Rien." The reading slows down or loops, performing an involuntary imitation of what the sentence says. As far as I know, only Gilles Deleuze vaunts the merits of variable speed in reading (even if, in the end, that reading is indexed on what the writing itself "demands"): "An author acknowledged as difficult generally demands to be read slowly: in this case [in Hélène Cixous' novel *Neutre*], however, the work asks us to read it 'fast,' and we are bound to read it again, faster and faster. The difficulties which a slower reader would experience dissolve as the

reading speed increases." "Hélène Cixous, or Writing in Strobe," in *Desert Islands and Other Texts*, trans. Michael Taormina (Los Angeles: Semiotext(e), 2004), p. 230.

10. Benjamin, "Doctrine of the Similar," p. 698.

11. Plato, *Phaedrus*, trans. H. N. Fowler (New York: G. P. Putnam's Sons, 1919), 262e, p. 525.

12. Italo Calvino, *If on a Winter's Night a Traveler*, trans. William Weaver (London: Vintage, 1998), p. 68.

13. Ibid., p. 72.

14. On BookTube and readathons, see Violaine Morin, "Le top départ du marathon lecture est donné sur YouTube," *Le Monde*, August 6, 2015. On silent book clubs during the coronavirus pandemic, see Victoria Namkung, "The Silent Book Club, a Global Meet-Up for Introverts, Now Connects Them Remotely," *Los Angeles Times*, April 10, 2020. Both of the jessethereader's videos I refer to, "The Many Faces of a Reader" and "Thoughts That Cross My Mind While Reading," can be found on YouTube.

15. Giorgio Agamben, *The Fire and the Tale*, trans. Lorenzo Chiesa (Stanford, CA: Stanford University Press, 2017), p. 102.

16. Ibid., p. 104. Agamben goes so far as to propose an interpretation of the *volumen*, the *codex*, and the computer screen in a "theological perspective": "For Jews the sacred text is a roll; for Christians it is a book ... the computer appears somewhere between ... a sort of Judeo-Christian hybrid—and this could only have contributed to its almost indisputable primacy" (pp. 103–104). On the *volume* and the *codex*, see Guiglielmo Cavallo and Roger Chartier's introduction to Guglielmo Cavallo and Roger Chartier, eds., *A History of Reading in the West*, trans. Lydia G. Cochrane (Amherst: University of Massachusetts Press, 2003), pp. 1–36. Jean-Luc Nancy distinguishes the figure of the book that "forms a volume" from the book that is "discontinuous and a sheaf of leaves." And these two intertwined bibliological figures ("there was already *codex* in the *volumen*, just as there remains some of the latter in the former") embody two reading regimes, or two relations to the written text: one tends to "transmute it into a unique ... substance," to pull it together or gather it in a systolic movement, while the other, on the contrary, makes it "lose the almost mute assurance of its compact consistency," fragmenting it into a diastolic separation. *On the Commerce of Thinking: Of Books and Bookstores*, trans. David Wills (New York: Fordham University Press, 2009), pp. 31–32.

17. Walter Benjamin, "Unpacking My Library: A Talk about Book Collecting," trans. Harry Zohn, in *Walter Benjamin: Selected Writings, Volume 2, 1927–1934*, p. 486.

18. Ibid.

19. Ibid., p. 492; Walter Benjamin, *Gesammelte Schriften*, ed. Rolf Tiedemann and Hermann Schweppenhäuser, 7 vols. (Frankfurt: Suhrkamp, 1972), vol. 4, p. 395.

20. Benjamin, "Unpacking My Library," p. 492, translation emended to that in *Illuminations*, ed. Hannah Arendt (New York: Schocken Books, 1968), p. 67.

21. Benjamin, "Unpacking My Library," p. 492.

22. Ibid., p. 487.

23. Ibid., p. 488.

24. Ibid., translation emended. The English translation here says the exact opposite of the original, omitting the negative: Benjamin says no book could enter that had *not* been read — "das ich nicht gelesen hatte." Benjamin, *Gesammelte Schriften*, vol. 4, p. 391

25. Benjamin, "Unpacking My Library," p. 490.

26. Maurice Blanchot, "Reading," in *The Space of Literature*, trans. Ann Smock (Lincoln: University of Nebraska Press, 1982), pp. 192–93.

27. As Jean-Christophe Bailly imagined, in a very Benjaminian vein, in his *Une nuit à la bibilothèque*, a play first performed in 1999, directed by Gilberte Tsaï. (The text was published by Bourgois in 2005.)

28. "The phenomenon of collecting loses its meaning as it loses its personal owner," says Benjamin, immediately adding that "only in extinction is the collector comprehended" (p. 67).

29. Paul Valéry, *"My Faust,"* in *Plays*, trans. David Paul and Robert Fitzgerald (New York: Pantheon Books, 1960), p. 121.

Zone Books series design by Bruce Mau

Image placement and production by Julie Fry

Typesetting by Meighan Gale

Printed and bound by Maple Press